KASPAR

DIANE OBOMSAWIN

DRAWN AND QUARTERLY

MONTREAL

PORTRAIT OF KASPAR HAUSER ON FRONT AND BACK ENDPAPERS IS A
REPRODUCTION OF A DRAWING BY PROFESSOR GEORG FRIEDRICH DAUMER.

TRANSLATION OF KASPAR HAUSER'S POEM ON PAGE 40: KATHLEEN OLIVER.

DRAWN AND QUARTERLY
POST OFFICE BOX 48056
MONTREAL, QUEBEC
CANADA H2V 4S8
WWW.DRAWNANDQUARTERLY.COM

FIRST EDITION: JANUARY 2009.
PRINTED IN CANADA.

10   9   8   7   6   5   4   3   2   1

LIBRARY AND ARCHIVES CANADA CATALOGUING IN PUBLICATION
KASPAR / AUTHOR/ARTIST: DIANE OBOMSAWIN ; TRANSLATOR: HELGE DASCHER.
TRANSLATION OF TITLE: KASPAR. (ORIGINALLY PUBLISHED IN FRENCH BY
L'OIE DE CRAVAN, MONTREAL, 2007.)
ISBN 978-1-897299-67-8
        I. DASCHER, HELGE, 1965-   II. TITLE.
PN6734.K36O26 2008   741.5'971   C2008-907003-8

DRAWN AND QUARTERLY ACKNOWLEDGES THE FINANCIAL CONTRIBUTION OF THE
GOVERNMENT OF CANADA THROUGH THE BOOK PUBLISHING INDUSTRY DEVELOP-
MENT PROGRAM (BPIDP) AND THE CANADA COUNCIL FOR THE ARTS FOR OUR
PUBLISHING ACTIVITIES AND FOR SUPPORT OF THIS EDITION.

DISTRIBUTED IN THE USA BY:
FARRAR, STRAUS AND GIROUX
18 WEST 18TH STREET
NEW YORK, NY 10011
ORDERS: 888.330.8477

DISTRIBUTED IN CANADA BY:
RAINCOAST BOOKS
9050 SHAUGHNESSY STREET
VANCOUVER, BC V6P 6E5
ORDERS: 800.663.5714

PRINTED BY IMPRIMERIE TRANSCONTINENTAL IN SHERBROOKE, QUEBEC,
JANUARY 2009.

TRANSLATED BY
HELGE DASCHER

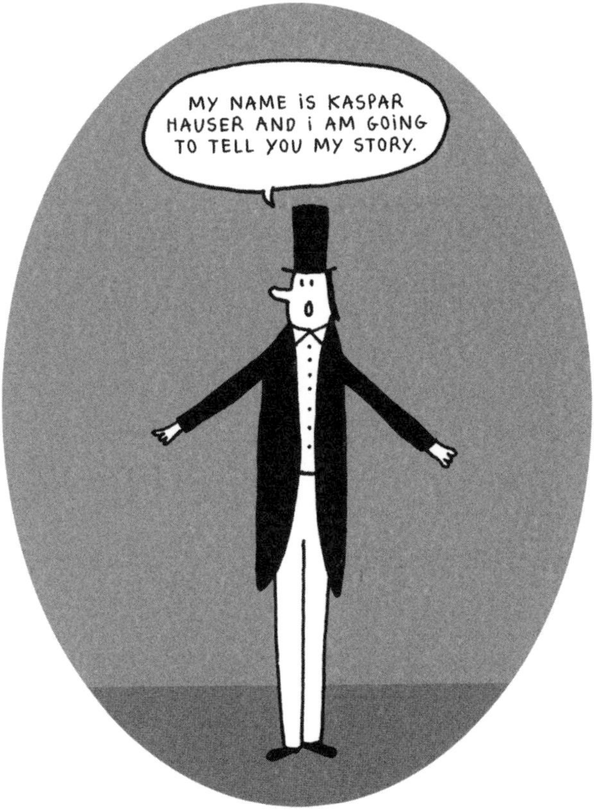
MY NAME IS KASPAR HAUSER AND I AM GOING TO TELL YOU MY STORY.

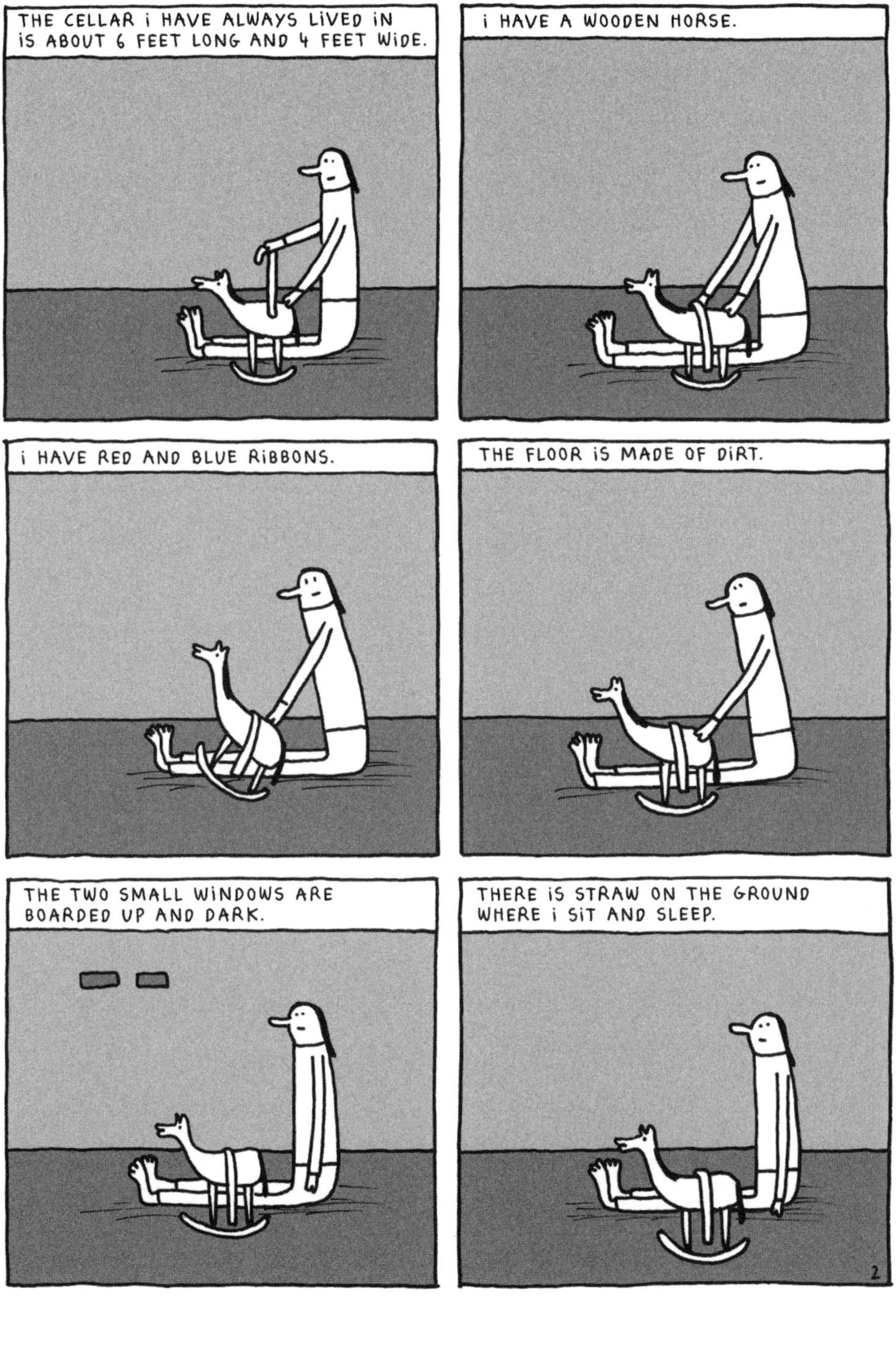
THE CELLAR i HAVE ALWAYS LiVED iN iS ABOUT 6 FEET LONG AND 4 FEET WiDE.
i HAVE A WOODEN HORSE.
i HAVE RED AND BLUE RiBBONS.
THE FLOOR iS MADE OF DiRT.
THE TWO SMALL WiNDOWS ARE BOARDED UP AND DARK.
THERE iS STRAW ON THE GROUND WHERE i SiT AND SLEEP.

IT NEVER OCCURS TO ME TO WANT TO STAND UP.

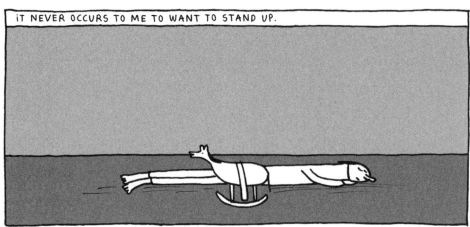

THERE IS A HOLE IN THE FLOOR WITH A BUCKET IN IT.

WHEN I WAKE UP THERE IS A PIECE OF BREAD AT MY SIDE...

...AND A LITTLE JUG OF WATER.

3

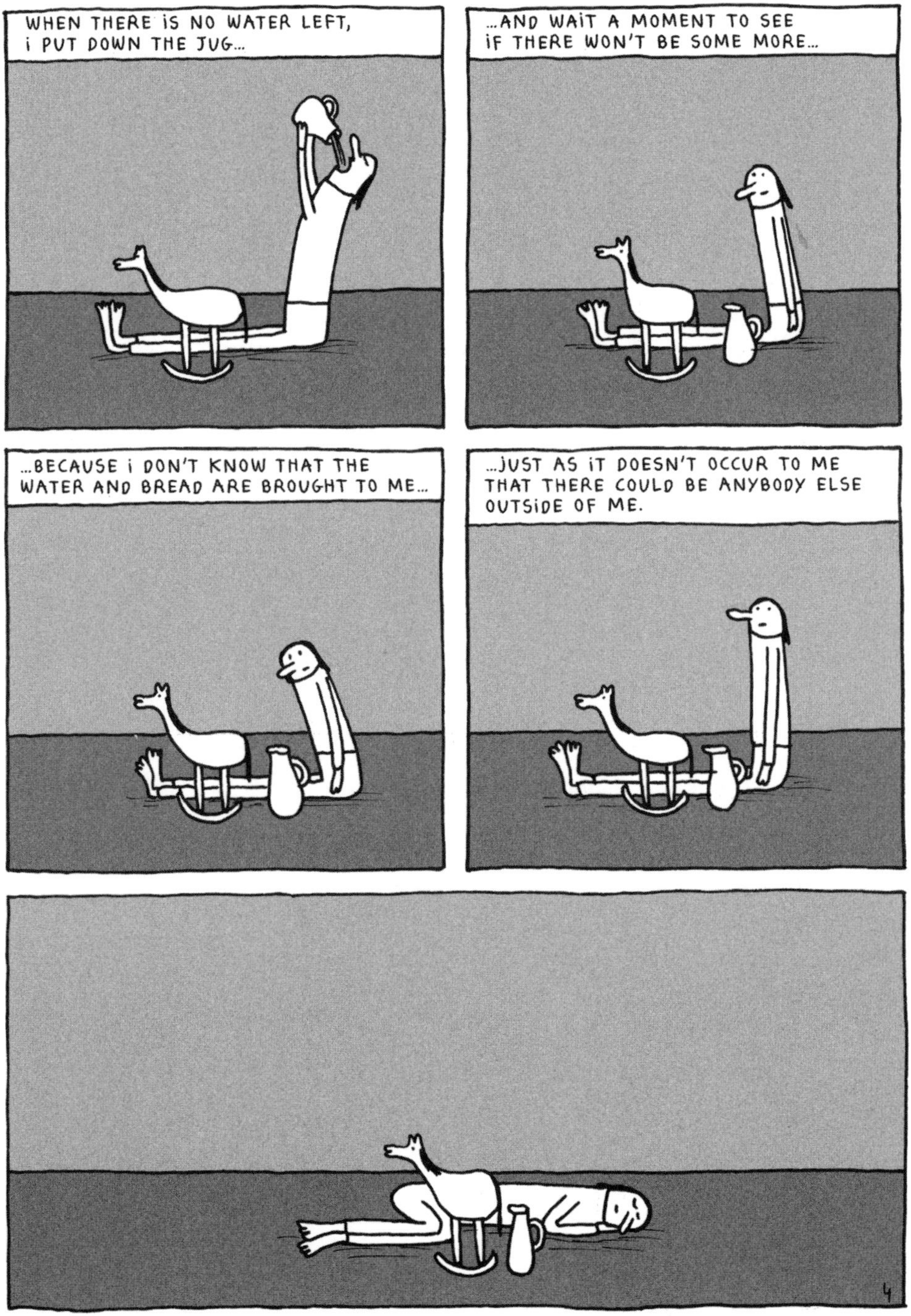
WHEN THERE IS NO WATER LEFT, I PUT DOWN THE JUG...
...AND WAIT A MOMENT TO SEE IF THERE WON'T BE SOME MORE...
...BECAUSE I DON'T KNOW THAT THE WATER AND BREAD ARE BROUGHT TO ME...
...JUST AS IT DOESN'T OCCUR TO ME THAT THERE COULD BE ANYBODY ELSE OUTSIDE OF ME.
4

ONE DAY A MAN IN BLACK APPEARS.

i WILL TEACH YOU TO WRITE!

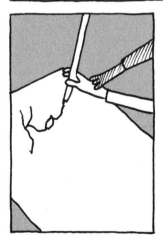

i NEVER HEAR HiM COME AND GO.

5

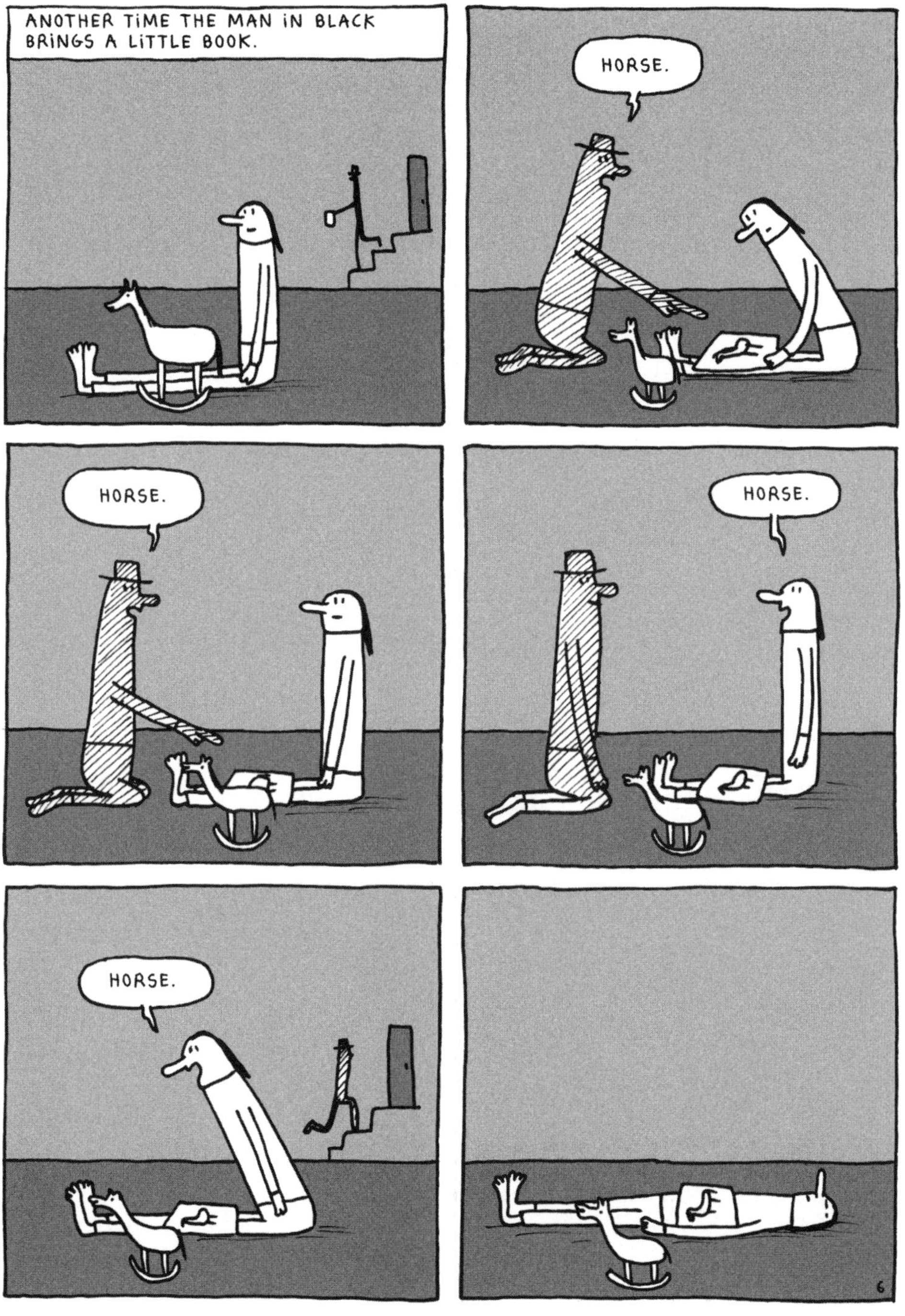
ANOTHER TIME THE MAN IN BLACK BRINGS A LITTLE BOOK.
HORSE.
HORSE.
HORSE.
HORSE.
6

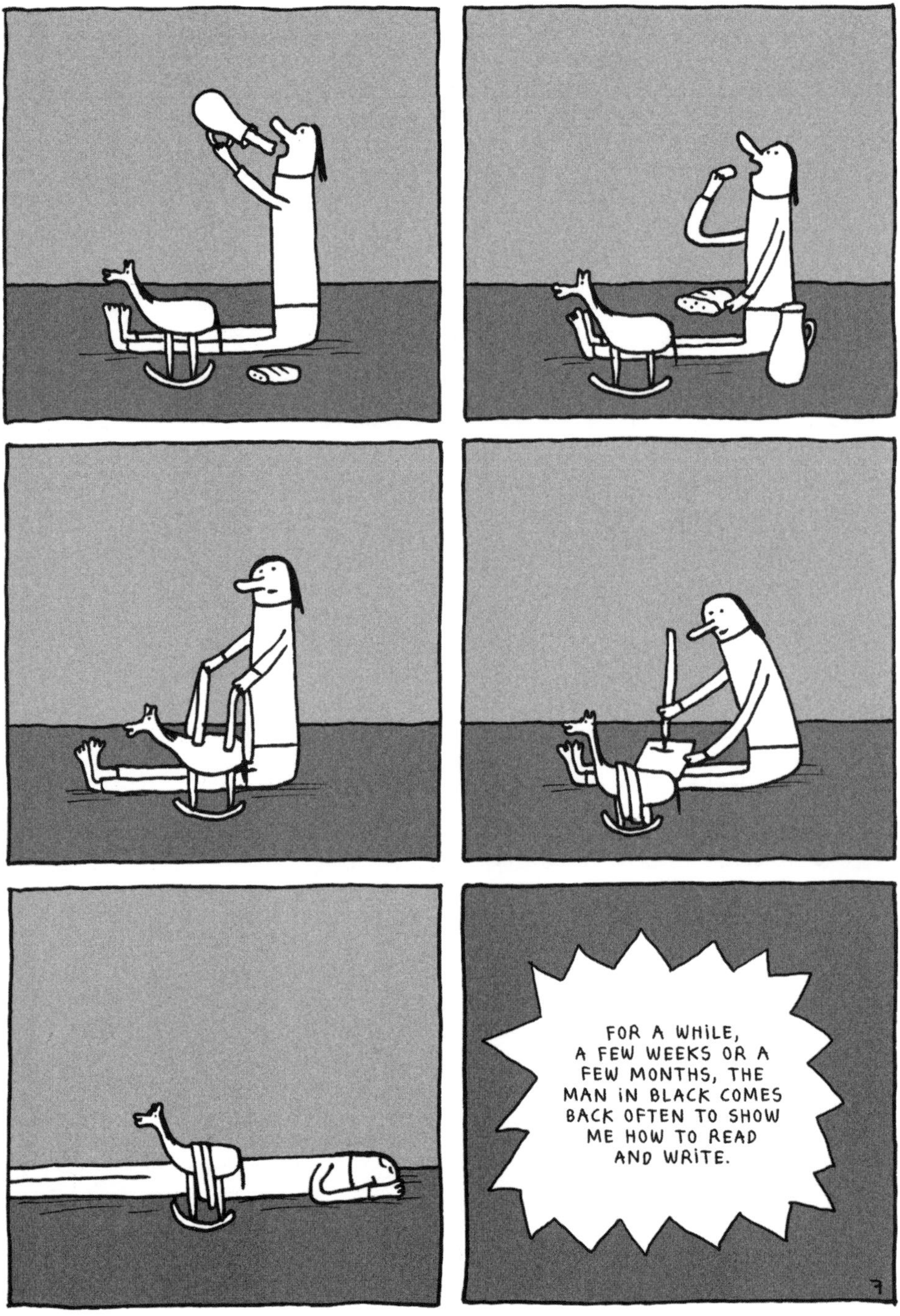
FOR A WHILE, A FEW WEEKS OR A FEW MONTHS, THE MAN IN BLACK COMES BACK OFTEN TO SHOW ME HOW TO READ AND WRITE.

THE NIGHT HE COMES TO GET ME, i'M SOUND ASLEEP.

HE PROPS ME UP AGAINST THE WALL.

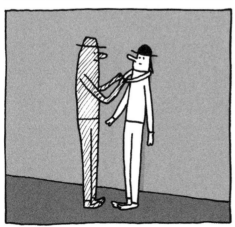

8

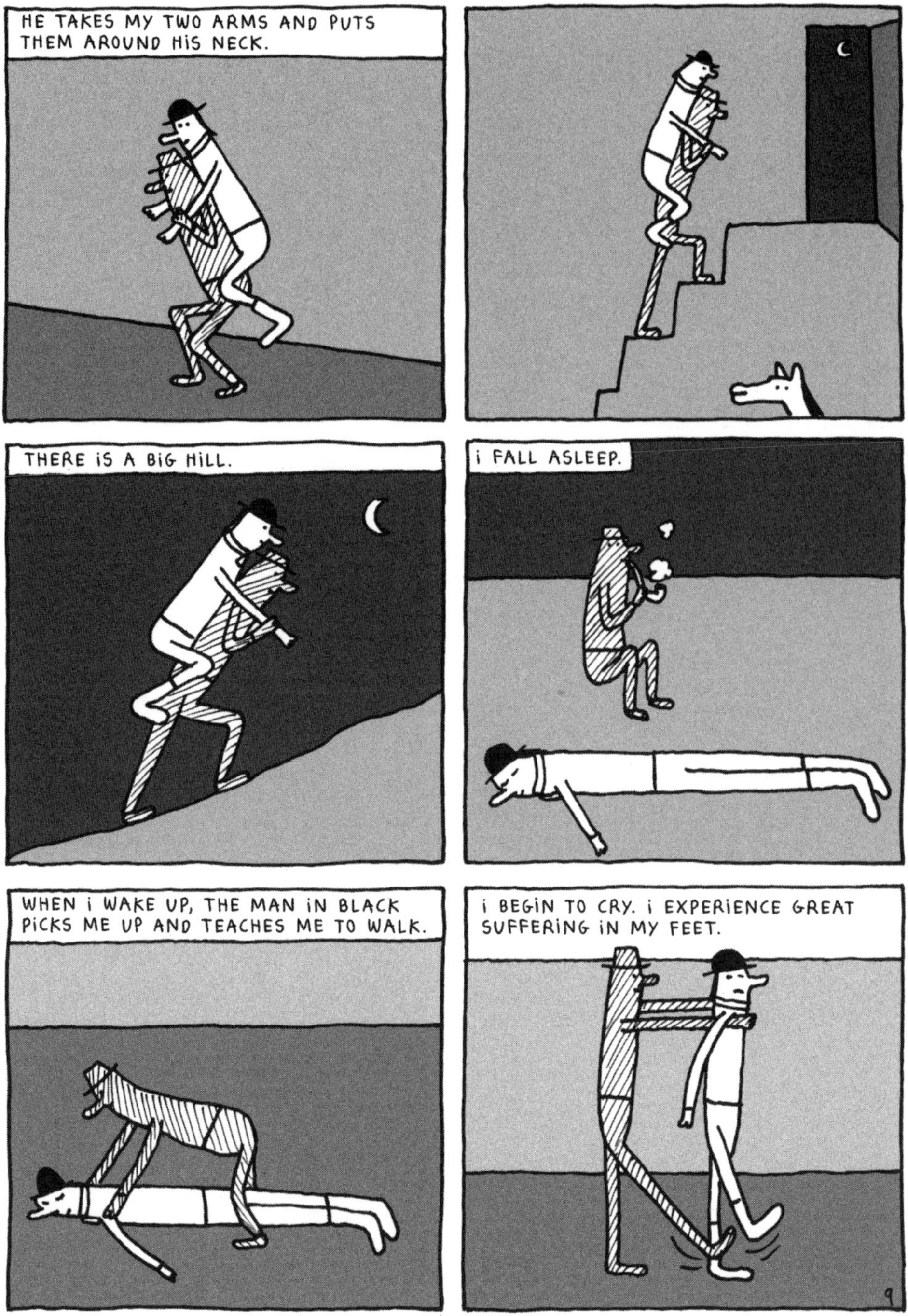
HE TAKES MY TWO ARMS AND PUTS THEM AROUND HIS NECK.
THERE IS A BIG HILL.
i FALL ASLEEP.
WHEN i WAKE UP, THE MAN iN BLACK PiCKS ME UP AND TEACHES ME TO WALK.
i BEGiN TO CRY. i EXPERiENCE GREAT SUFFERiNG iN MY FEET.

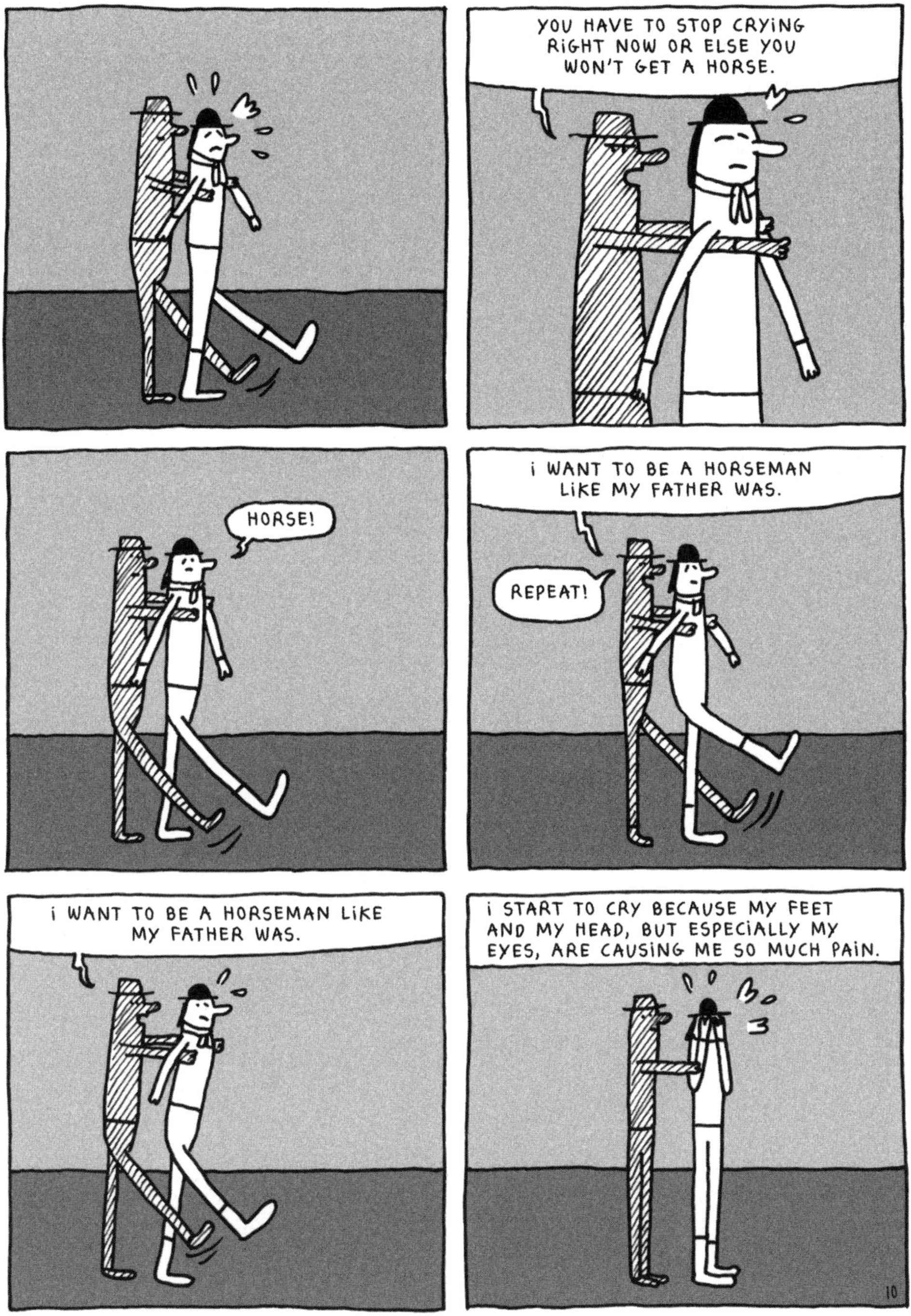
YOU HAVE TO STOP CRYING RIGHT NOW OR ELSE YOU WON'T GET A HORSE.
HORSE!
I WANT TO BE A HORSEMAN LIKE MY FATHER WAS.
REPEAT!
I WANT TO BE A HORSEMAN LIKE MY FATHER WAS.
I START TO CRY BECAUSE MY FEET AND MY HEAD, BUT ESPECIALLY MY EYES, ARE CAUSING ME SO MUCH PAIN.

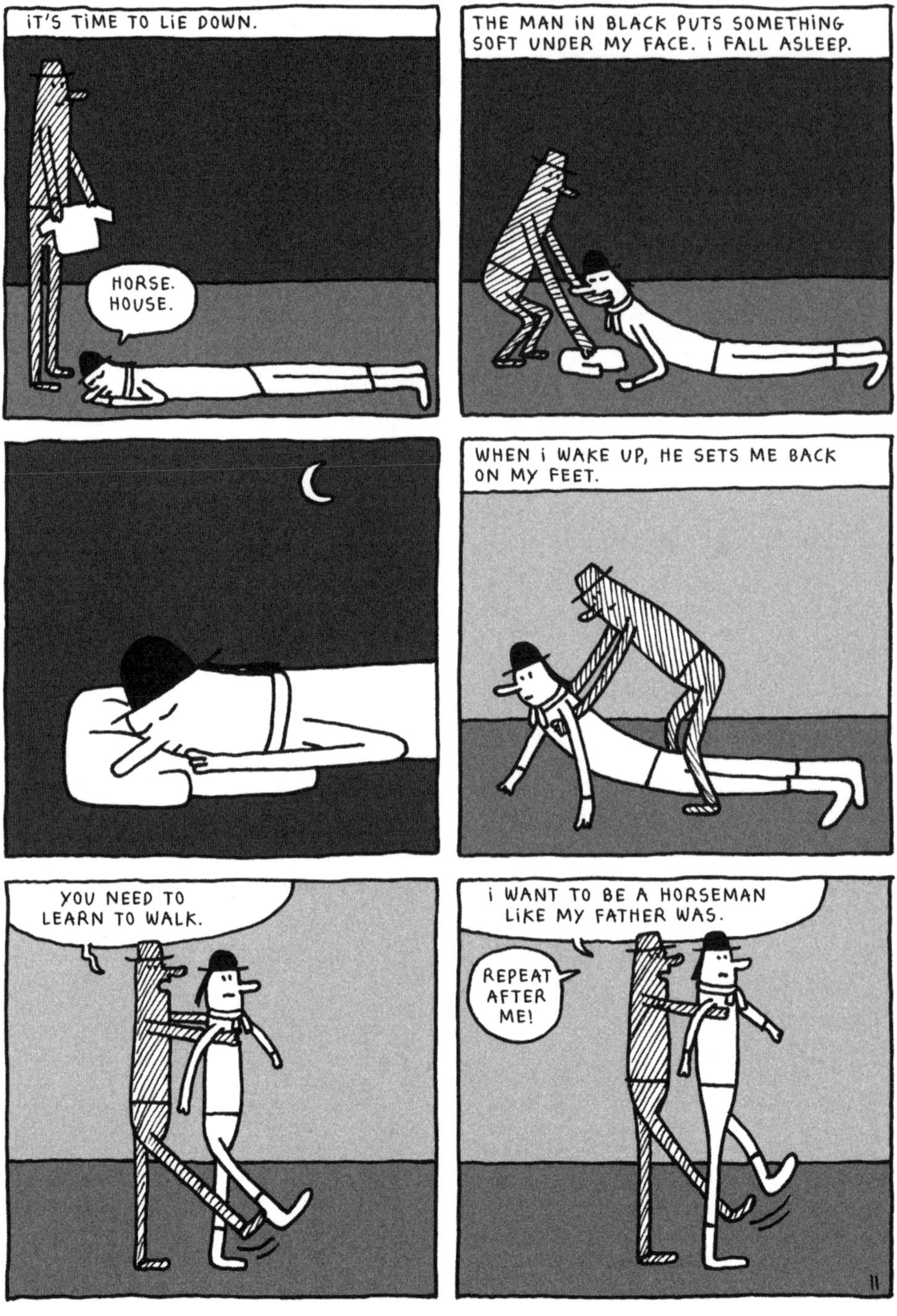
iT'S TiME TO LiE DOWN.
HORSE. HOUSE.
THE MAN iN BLACK PUTS SOMETHiNG SOFT UNDER MY FACE. i FALL ASLEEP.
WHEN i WAKE UP, HE SETS ME BACK ON MY FEET.
YOU NEED TO LEARN TO WALK.
i WANT TO BE A HORSEMAN LiKE MY FATHER WAS.
REPEAT AFTER ME!

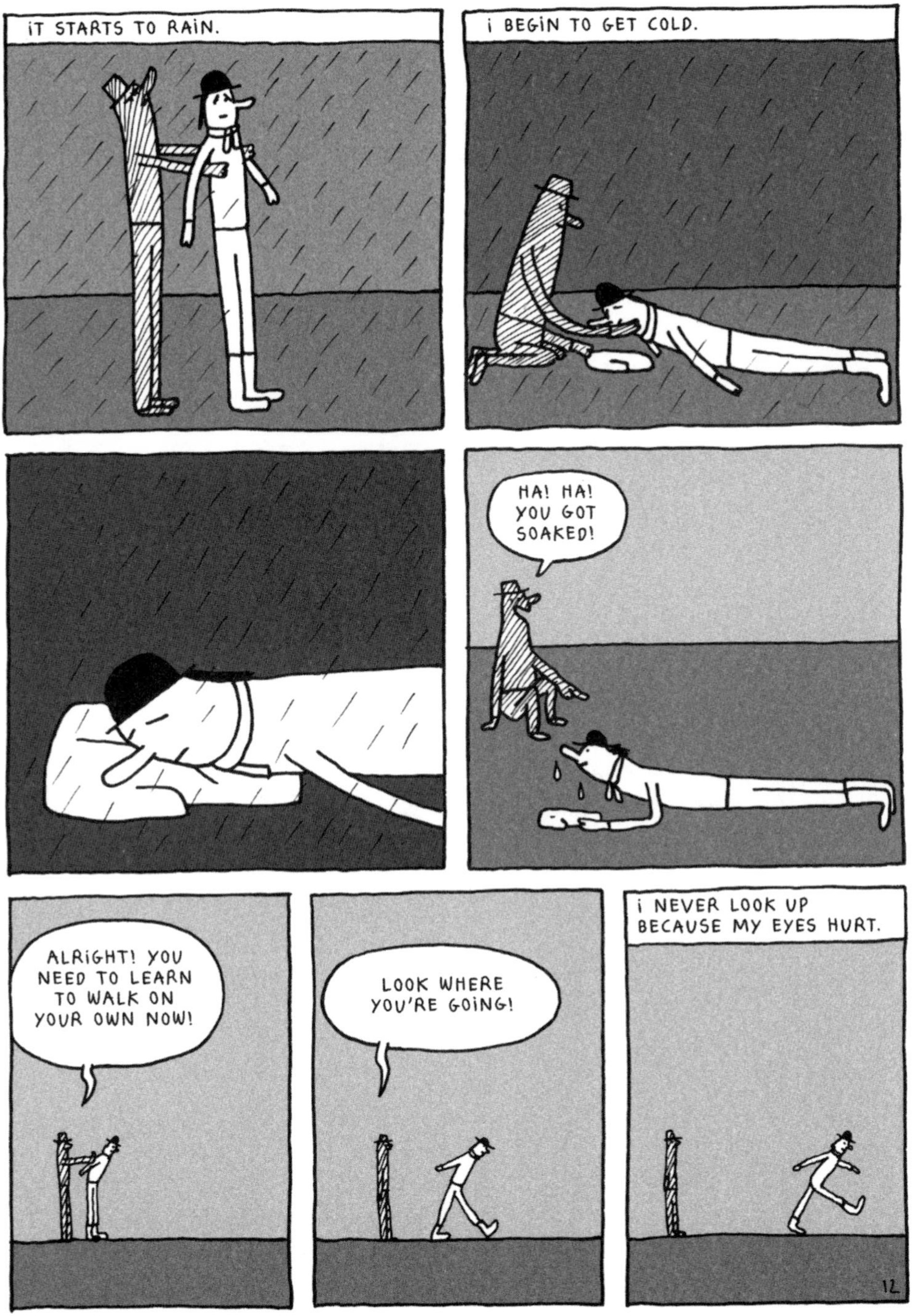
iT STARTS TO RAiN.
i BEGiN TO GET COLD.
HA! HA! YOU GOT SOAKED!
ALRiGHT! YOU NEED TO LEARN TO WALK ON YOUR OWN NOW!
LOOK WHERE YOU'RE GOiNG!
i NEVER LOOK UP BECAUSE MY EYES HURT.
12

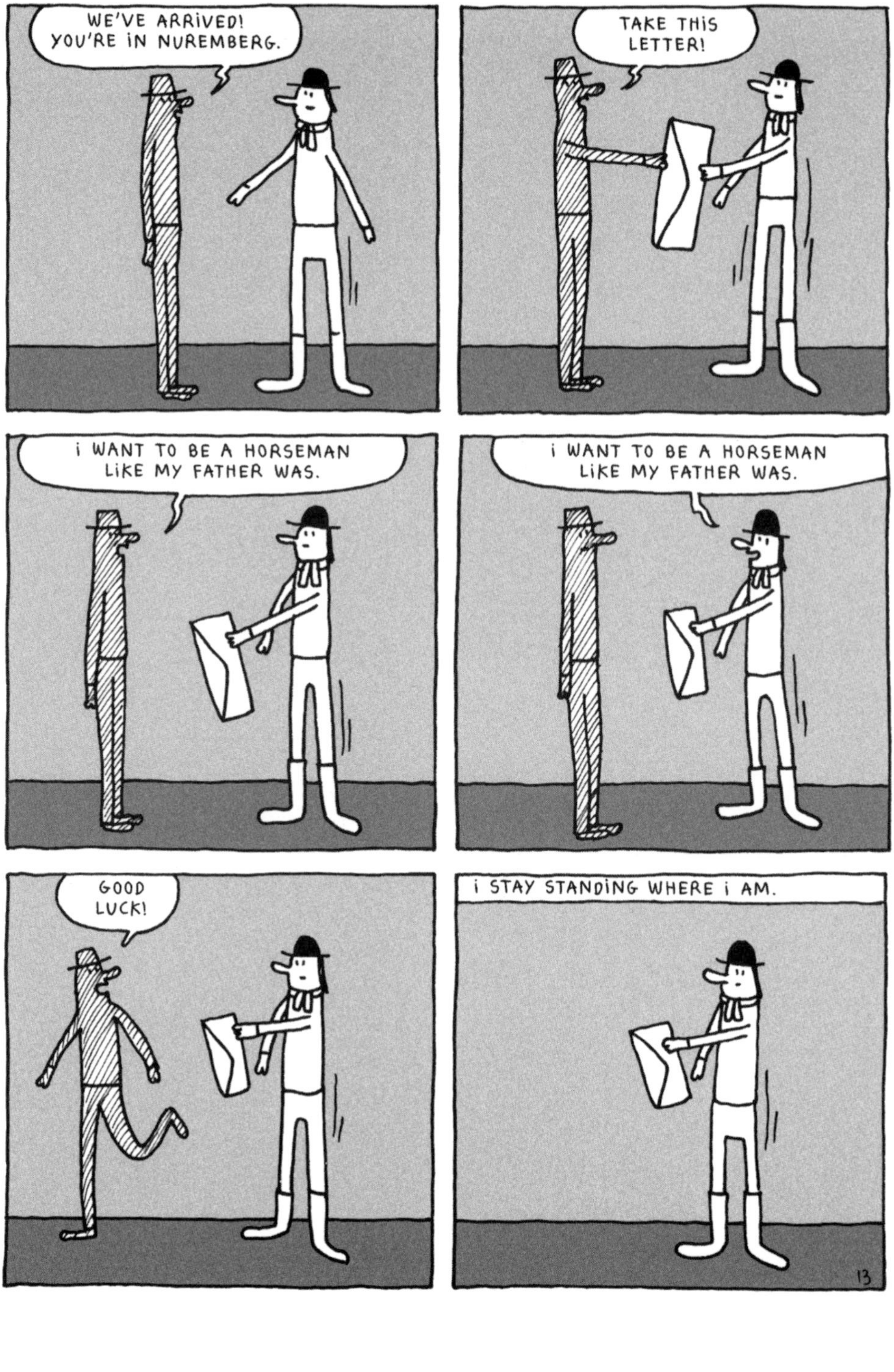
WE'VE ARRIVED! YOU'RE IN NUREMBERG.
TAKE THIS LETTER!
I WANT TO BE A HORSEMAN LIKE MY FATHER WAS.
I WANT TO BE A HORSEMAN LIKE MY FATHER WAS.
GOOD LUCK!
I STAY STANDING WHERE I AM.

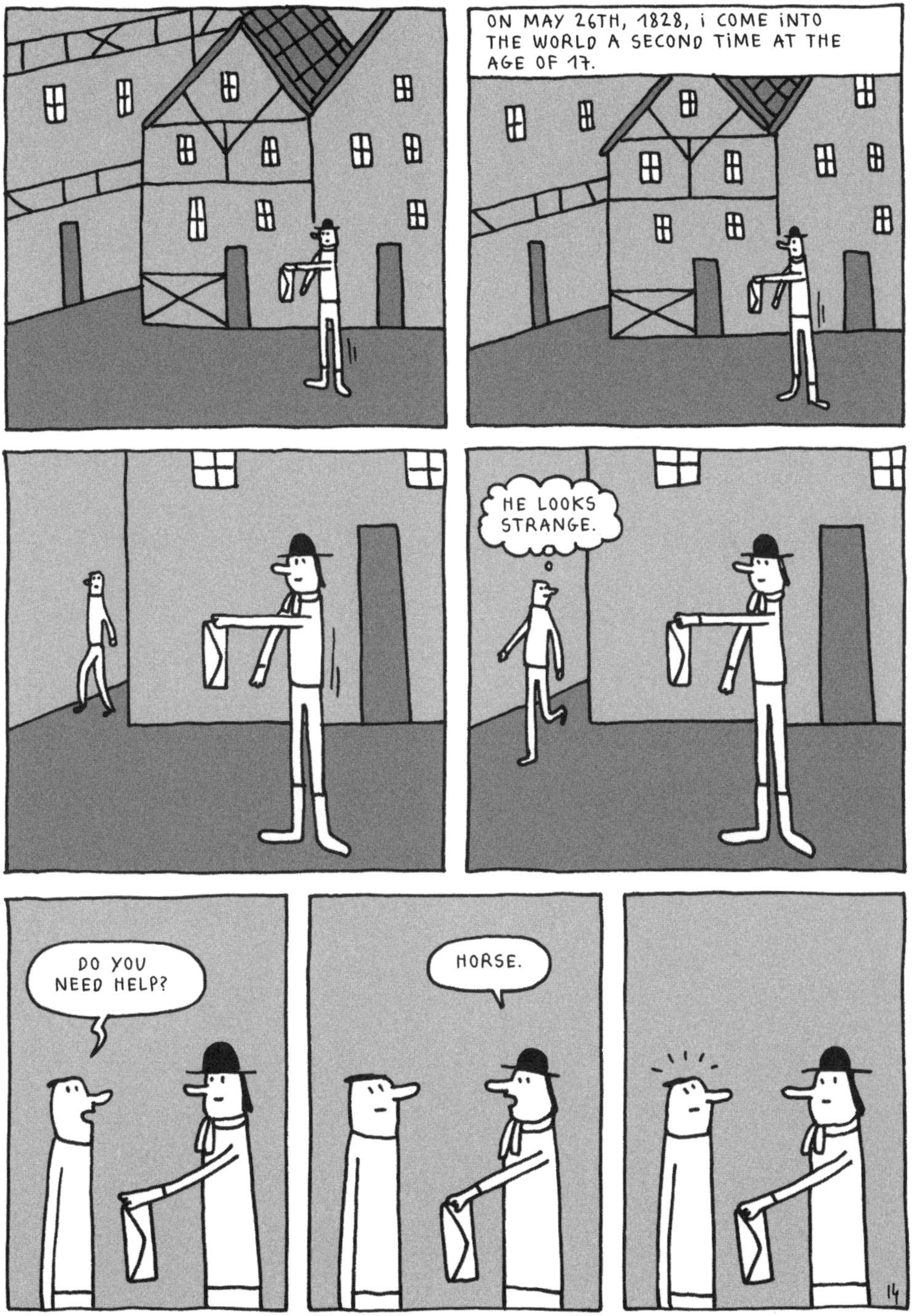
ON MAY 26TH, 1828, i COME iNTO THE WORLD A SECOND TiME AT THE AGE OF 17.
HE LOOKS STRANGE.
DO YOU NEED HELP?
HORSE.

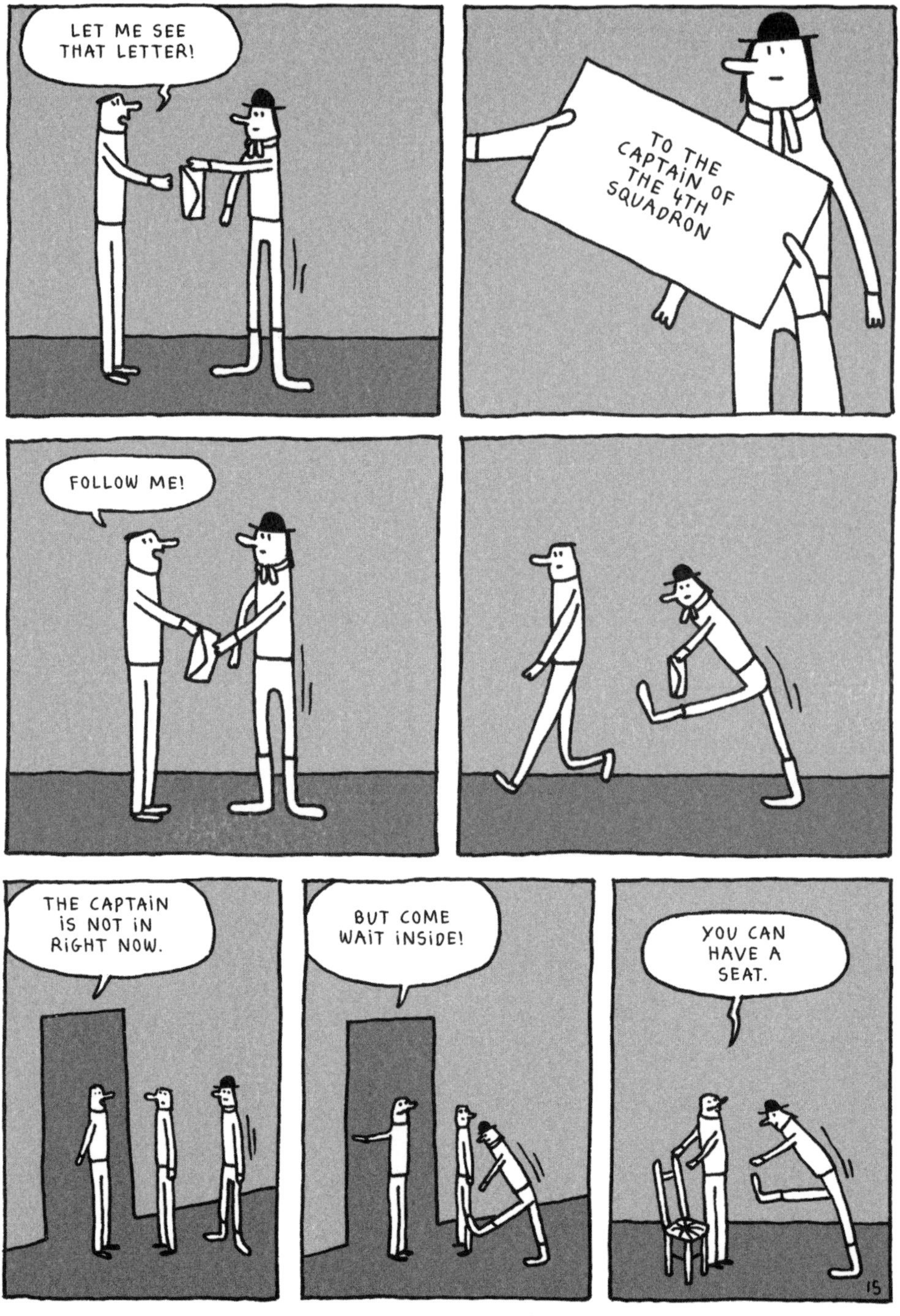
LET ME SEE THAT LETTER!
TO THE CAPTAIN OF THE 4TH SQUADRON
FOLLOW ME!
THE CAPTAIN IS NOT IN RIGHT NOW.
BUT COME WAIT INSIDE!
YOU CAN HAVE A SEAT.

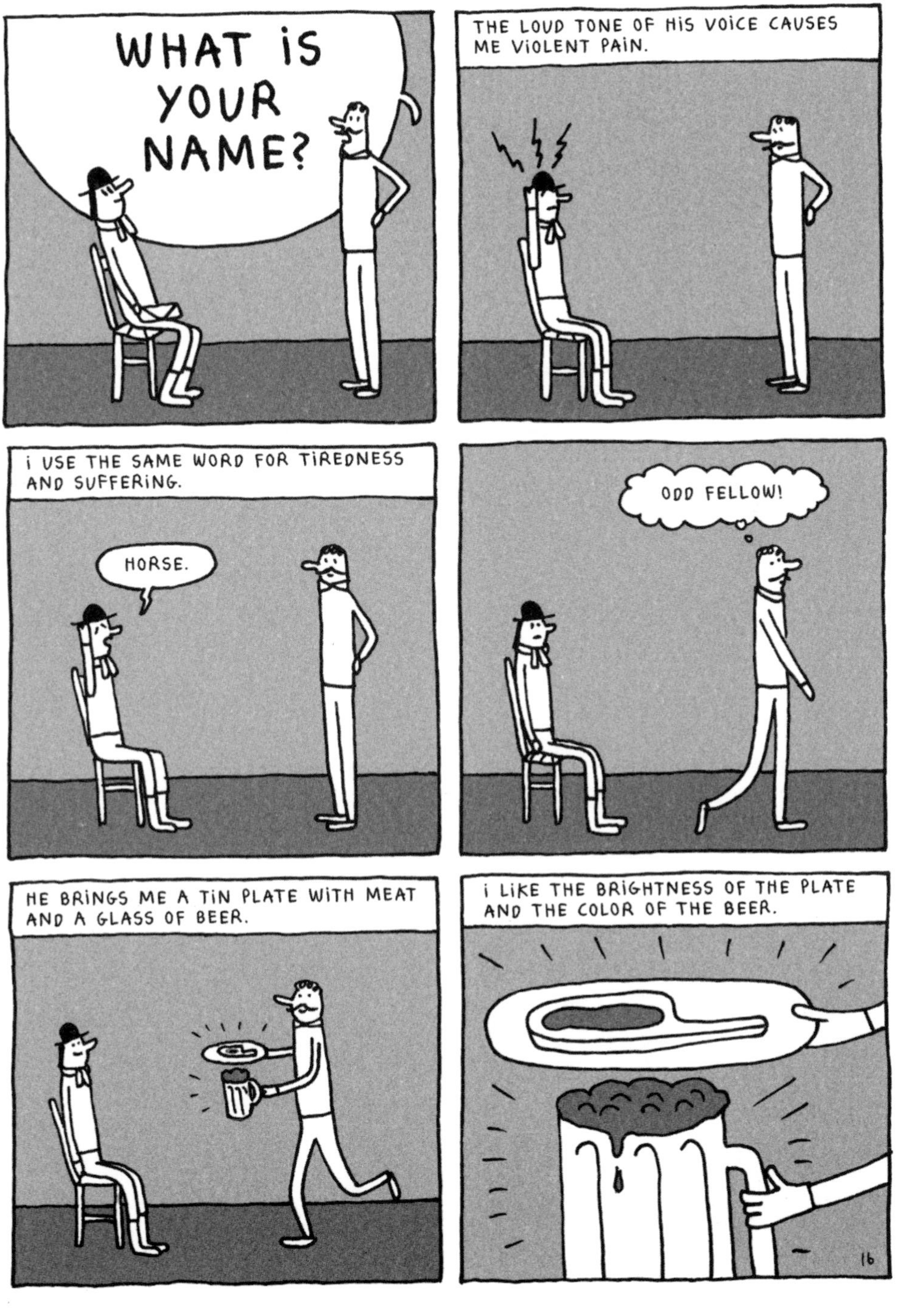
WHAT iS YOUR NAME?
THE LOUD TONE OF HiS VOiCE CAUSES ME ViOLENT PAiN.
i USE THE SAME WORD FOR TiREDNESS AND SUFFERiNG.
HORSE.
ODD FELLOW!
HE BRiNGS ME A TiN PLATE WiTH MEAT AND A GLASS OF BEER.
i LiKE THE BRiGHTNESS OF THE PLATE AND THE COLOR OF THE BEER.

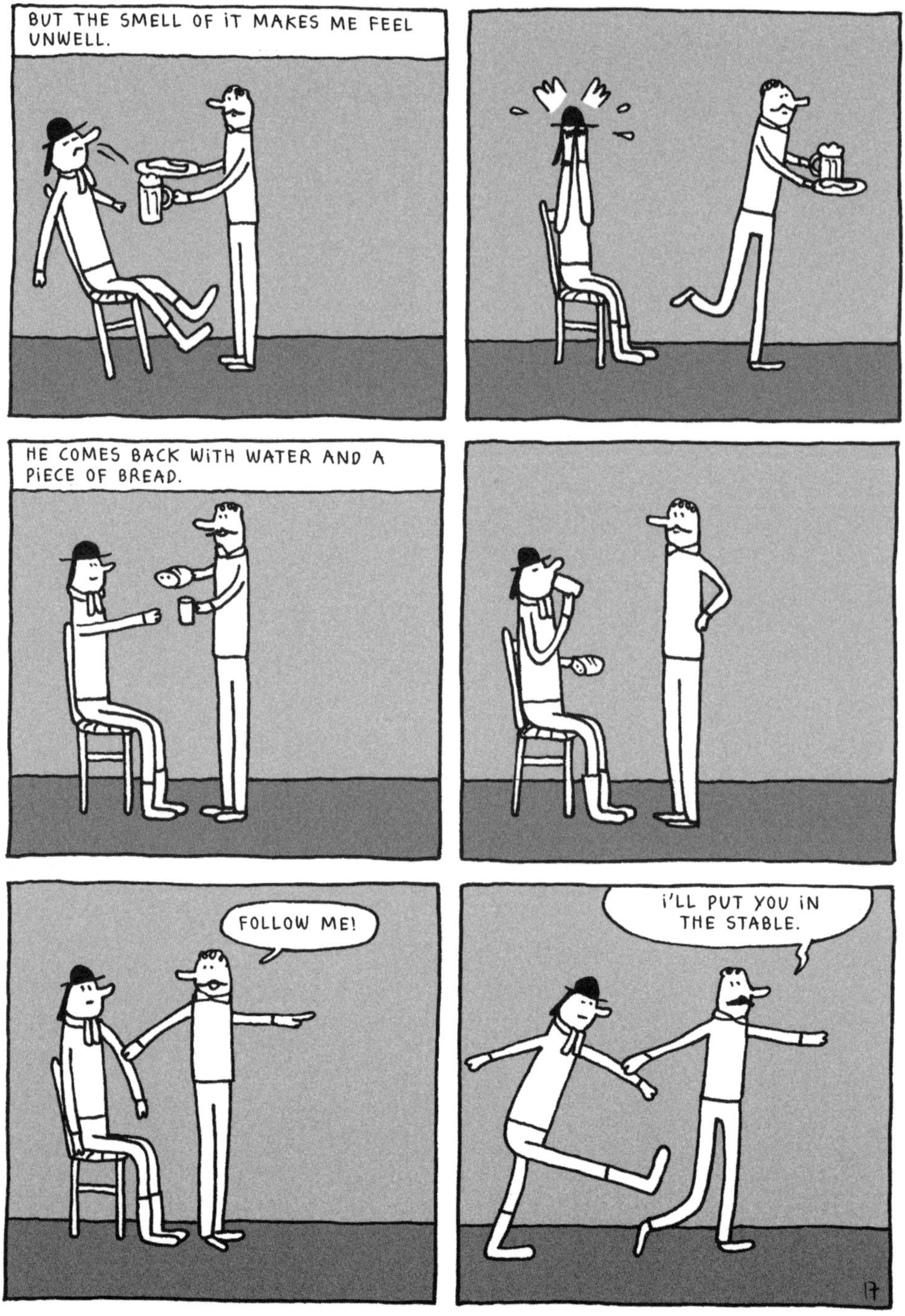
BUT THE SMELL OF iT MAKES ME FEEL UNWELL.
HE COMES BACK WiTH WATER AND A PiECE OF BREAD.
FOLLOW ME!
i'LL PUT YOU iN THE STABLE.

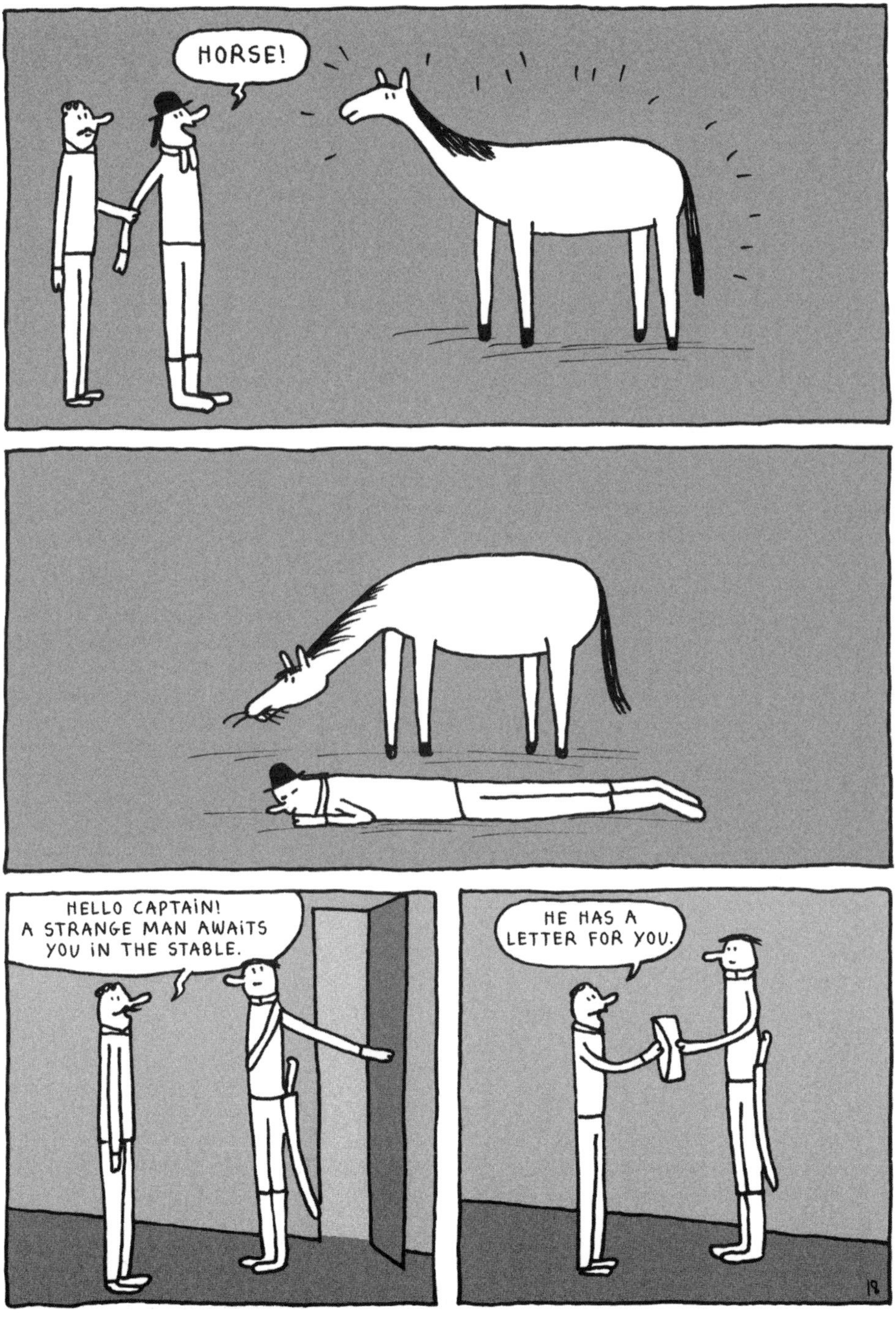
HORSE!
HELLO CAPTAIN! A STRANGE MAN AWAITS YOU IN THE STABLE.
HE HAS A LETTER FOR YOU.

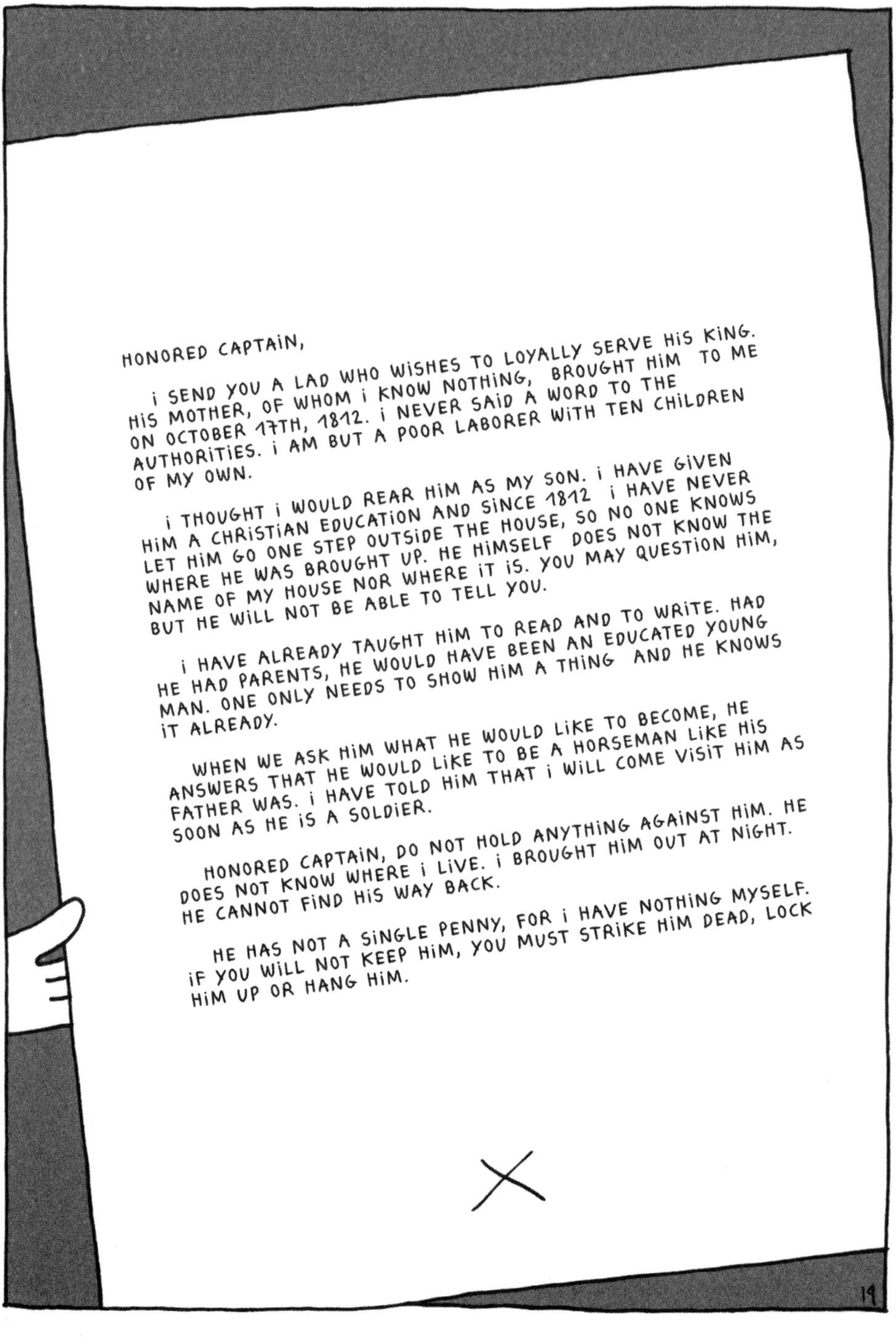

HONORED CAPTAIN,

i SEND YOU A LAD WHO WISHES TO LOYALLY SERVE HIS KING. HIS MOTHER, OF WHOM i KNOW NOTHING, BROUGHT HIM TO ME ON OCTOBER 17TH, 1812. i NEVER SAID A WORD TO THE AUTHORITIES. i AM BUT A POOR LABORER WITH TEN CHILDREN OF MY OWN.

i THOUGHT i WOULD REAR HIM AS MY SON. i HAVE GIVEN HIM A CHRISTIAN EDUCATION AND SINCE 1812 i HAVE NEVER LET HIM GO ONE STEP OUTSIDE THE HOUSE, SO NO ONE KNOWS WHERE HE WAS BROUGHT UP. HE HIMSELF DOES NOT KNOW THE NAME OF MY HOUSE NOR WHERE IT IS. YOU MAY QUESTION HIM, BUT HE WILL NOT BE ABLE TO TELL YOU.

i HAVE ALREADY TAUGHT HIM TO READ AND TO WRITE. HAD HE HAD PARENTS, HE WOULD HAVE BEEN AN EDUCATED YOUNG MAN. ONE ONLY NEEDS TO SHOW HIM A THING AND HE KNOWS IT ALREADY.

WHEN WE ASK HIM WHAT HE WOULD LIKE TO BECOME, HE ANSWERS THAT HE WOULD LIKE TO BE A HORSEMAN LIKE HIS FATHER WAS. i HAVE TOLD HIM THAT i WILL COME VISIT HIM AS SOON AS HE IS A SOLDIER.

HONORED CAPTAIN, DO NOT HOLD ANYTHING AGAINST HIM. HE DOES NOT KNOW WHERE i LIVE. i BROUGHT HIM OUT AT NIGHT. HE CANNOT FIND HIS WAY BACK.

HE HAS NOT A SINGLE PENNY, FOR i HAVE NOTHING MYSELF. IF YOU WILL NOT KEEP HIM, YOU MUST STRIKE HIM DEAD, LOCK HIM UP OR HANG HIM.

X

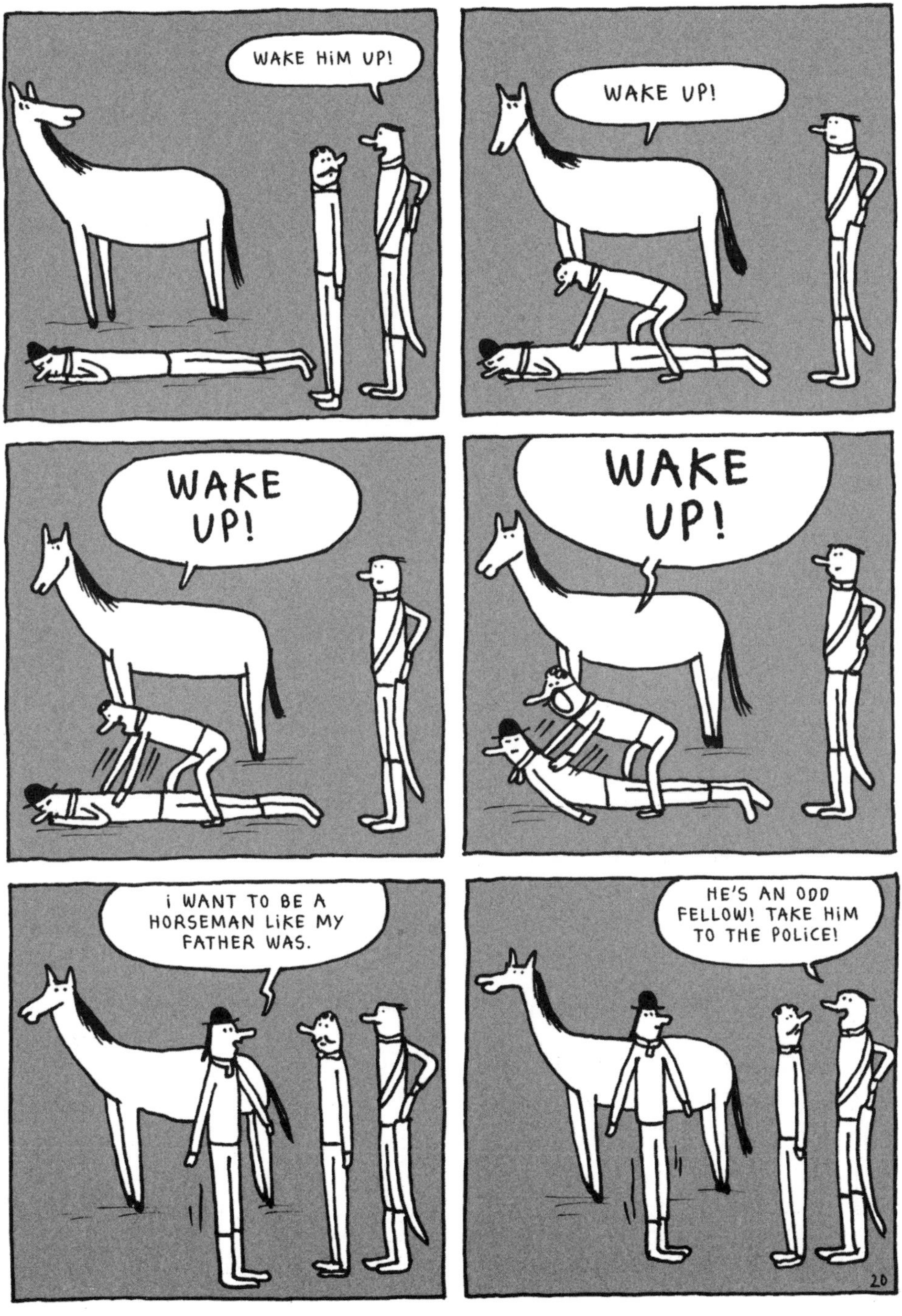
WAKE HIM UP!
WAKE UP!
WAKE UP!
WAKE UP!
I WANT TO BE A HORSEMAN LIKE MY FATHER WAS.
HE'S AN ODD FELLOW! TAKE HIM TO THE POLICE!
20

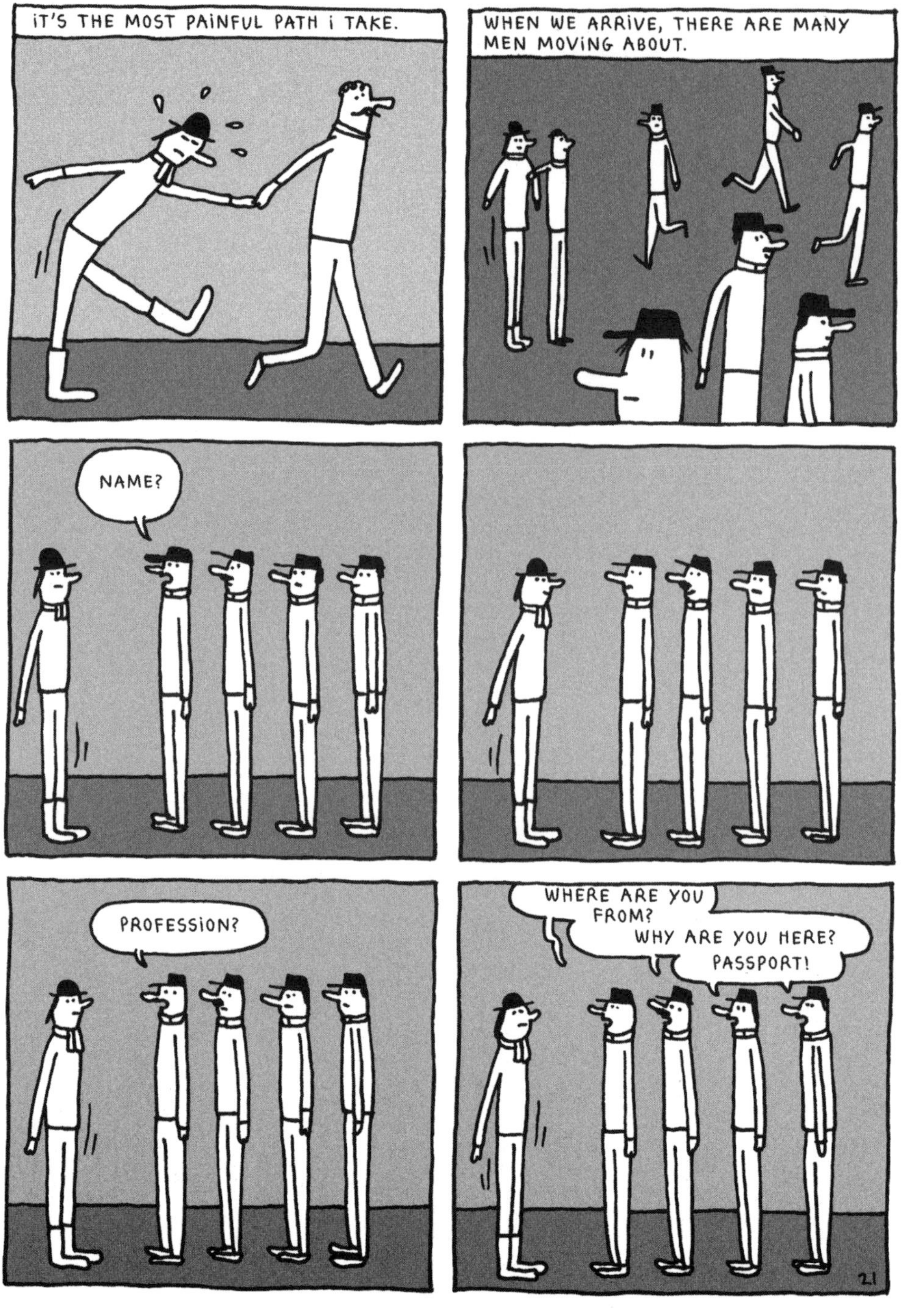

IT'S THE MOST PAINFUL PATH I TAKE.
WHEN WE ARRIVE, THERE ARE MANY MEN MOVING ABOUT.
NAME?
PROFESSION?
WHERE ARE YOU FROM?
WHY ARE YOU HERE?
PASSPORT!

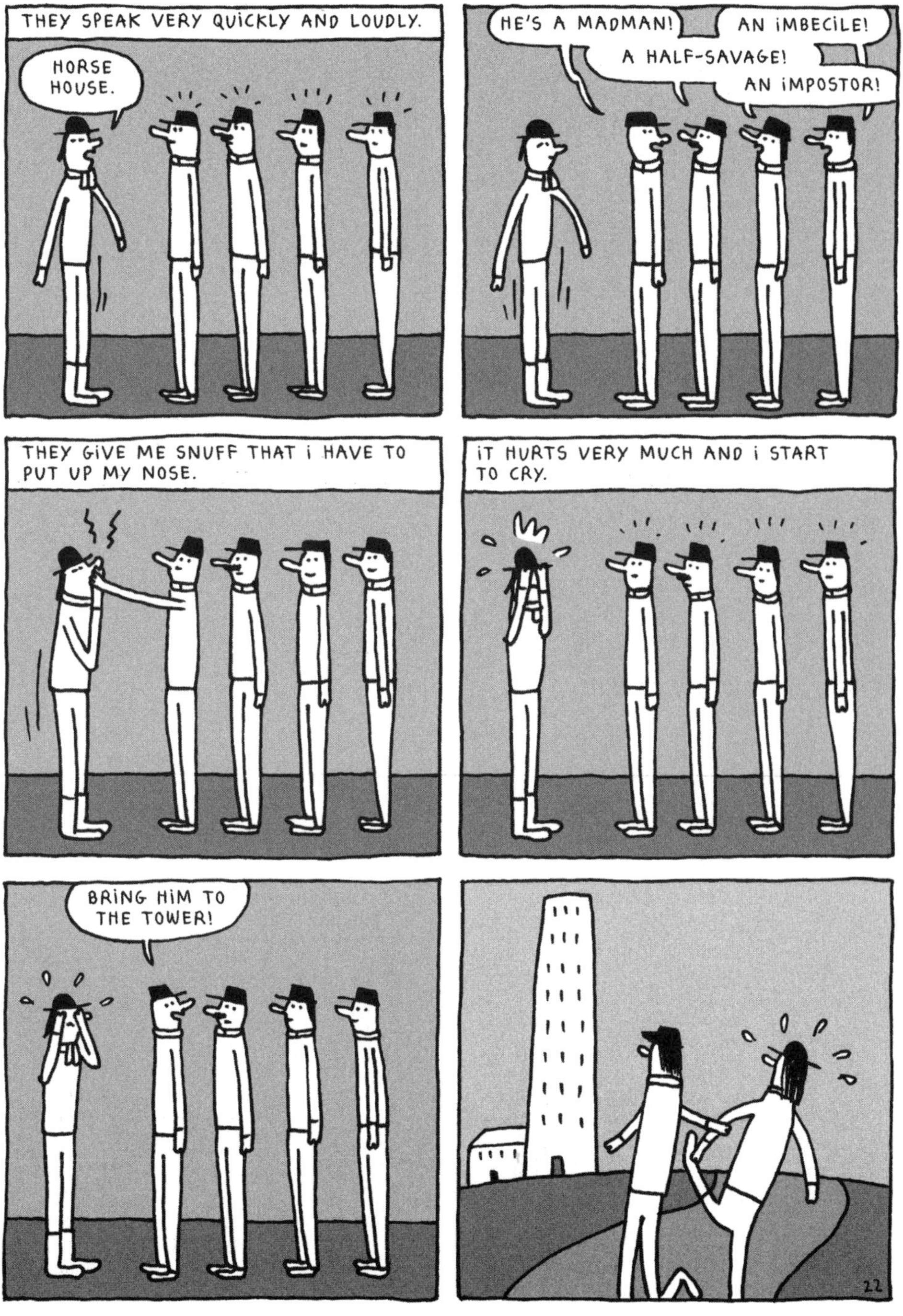
THEY SPEAK VERY QUICKLY AND LOUDLY.
HORSE HOUSE.
HE'S A MADMAN!
AN iMBECiLE!
A HALF-SAVAGE!
AN iMPOSTOR!
THEY GiVE ME SNUFF THAT i HAVE TO PUT UP MY NOSE.
iT HURTS VERY MUCH AND i START TO CRY.
BRiNG HiM TO THE TOWER!

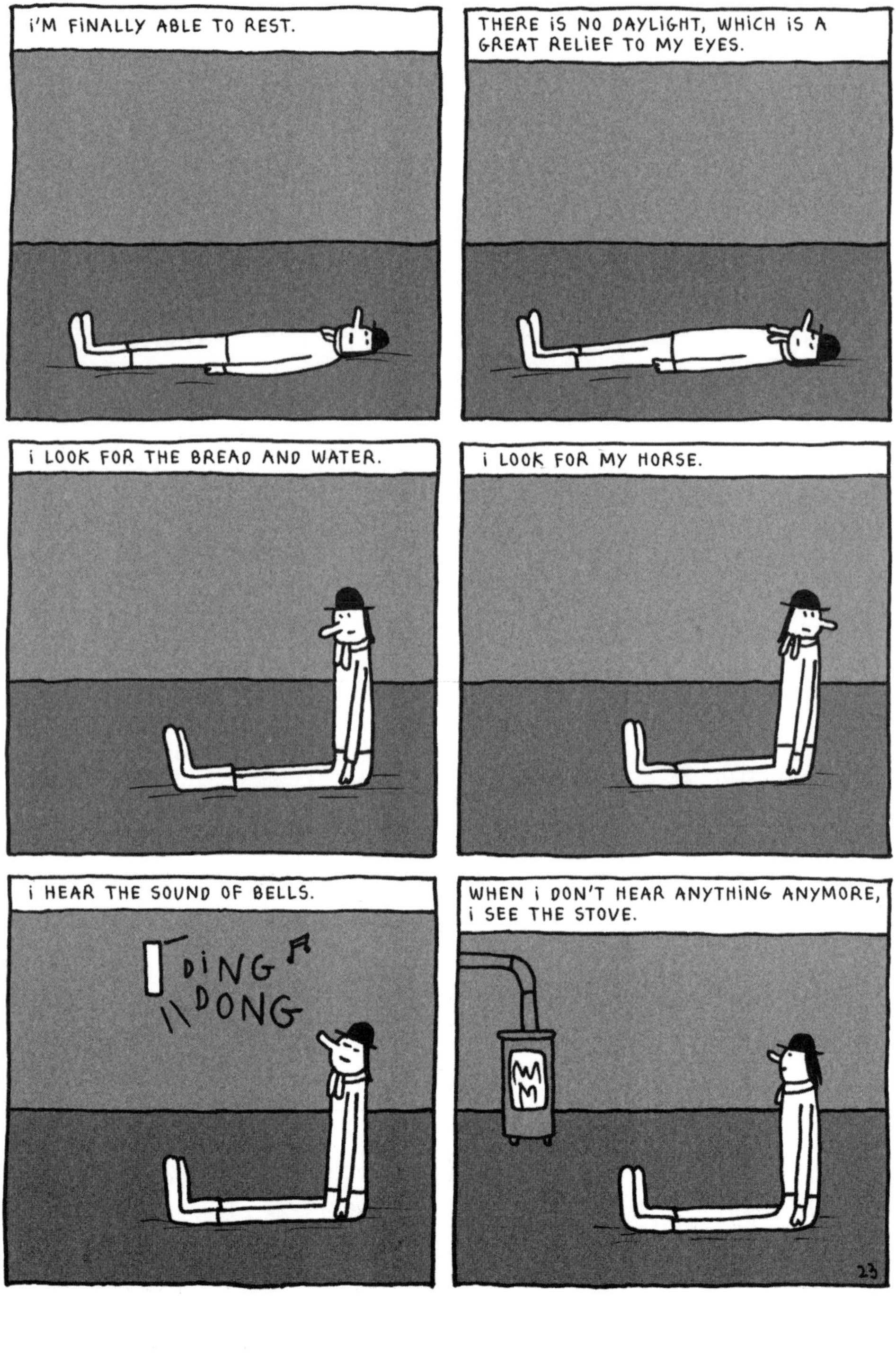
I'M FINALLY ABLE TO REST.
THERE IS NO DAYLIGHT, WHICH IS A GREAT RELIEF TO MY EYES.
I LOOK FOR THE BREAD AND WATER.
I LOOK FOR MY HORSE.
I HEAR THE SOUND OF BELLS.
DING
DONG
WHEN I DON'T HEAR ANYTHING ANYMORE, I SEE THE STOVE.

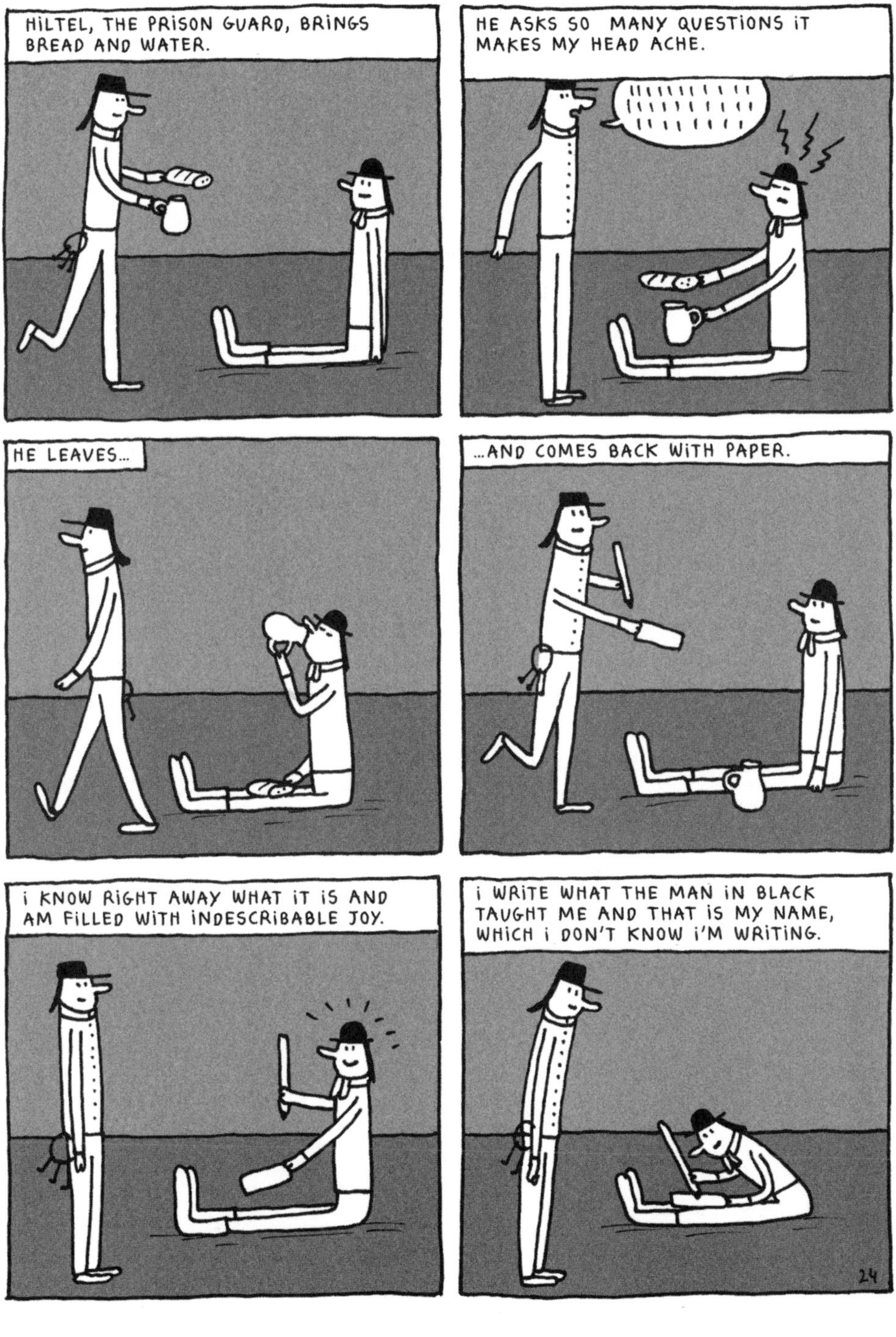
HILTEL, THE PRISON GUARD, BRINGS BREAD AND WATER.
HE ASKS SO MANY QUESTIONS IT MAKES MY HEAD ACHE.
HE LEAVES...
...AND COMES BACK WITH PAPER.
I KNOW RIGHT AWAY WHAT IT IS AND AM FILLED WITH INDESCRIBABLE JOY.
I WRITE WHAT THE MAN IN BLACK TAUGHT ME AND THAT IS MY NAME, WHICH I DON'T KNOW I'M WRITING.
24

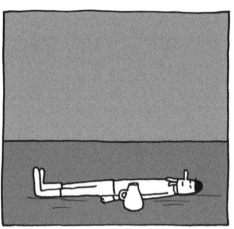

THE LIGHT BURNS MY EYES.

MY WIFE WILL GIVE YOU A NICE WARM BATH.

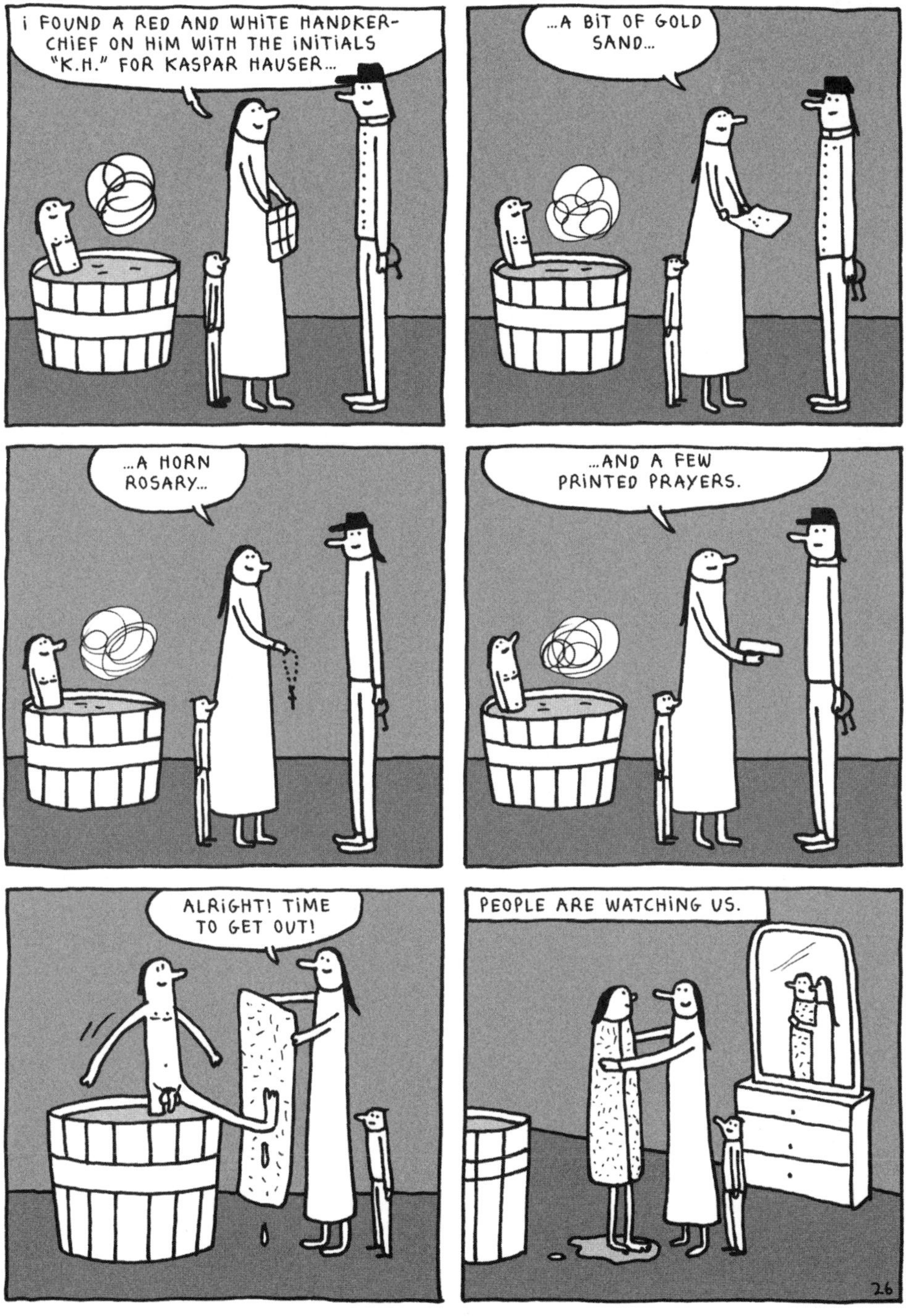

i FOUND A RED AND WHITE HANDKERCHIEF ON HiM WiTH THE iNiTiALS "K.H." FOR KASPAR HAUSER...
...A BiT OF GOLD SAND...
...A HORN ROSARY...
...AND A FEW PRiNTED PRAYERS.
ALRiGHT! TiME TO GET OUT!
PEOPLE ARE WATCHiNG US.

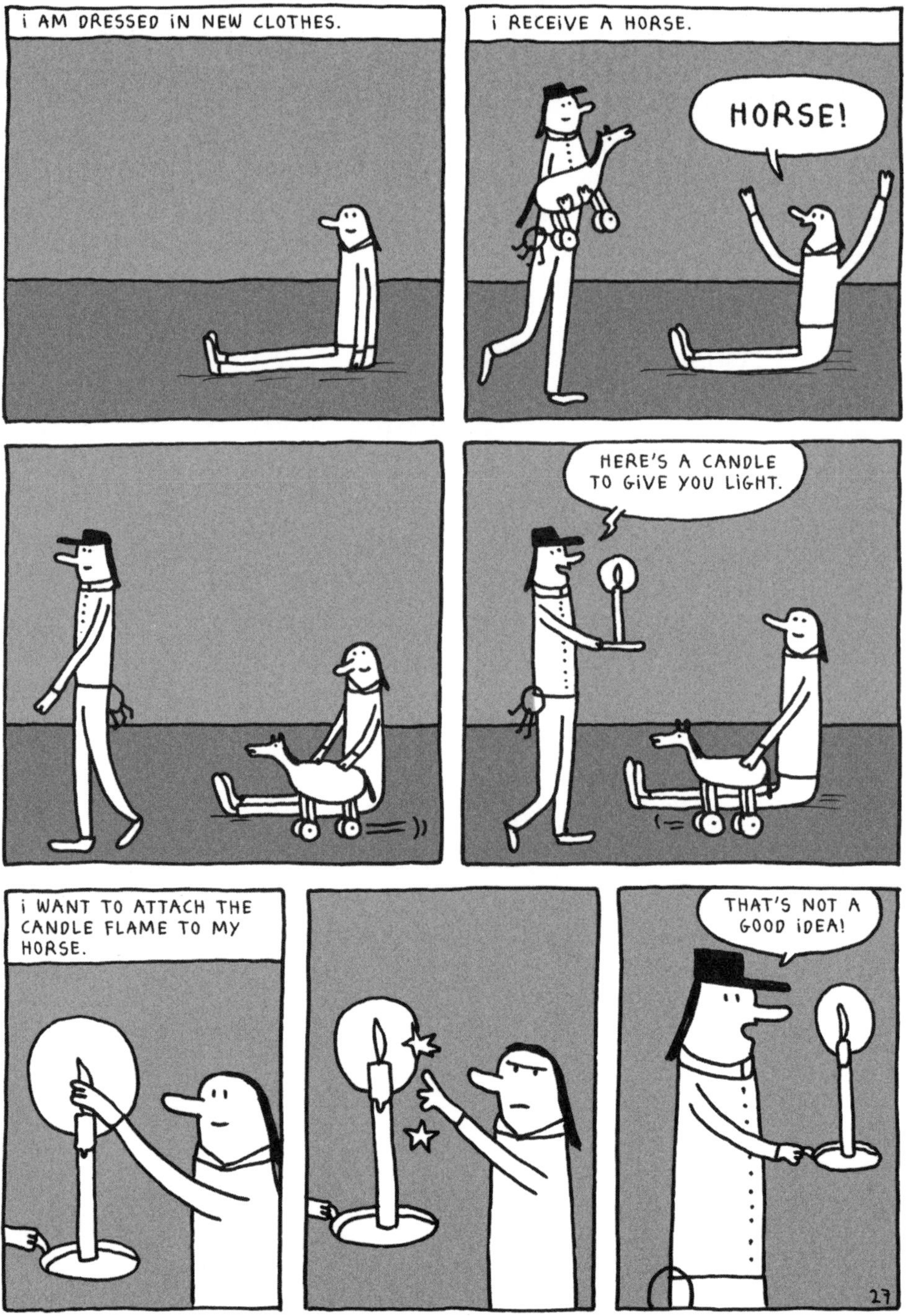
i AM DRESSED iN NEW CLOTHES.
i RECEiVE A HORSE.
HORSE!
HERE'S A CANDLE TO GiVE YOU LiGHT.
i WANT TO ATTACH THE CANDLE FLAME TO MY HORSE.
THAT'S NOT A GOOD iDEA!

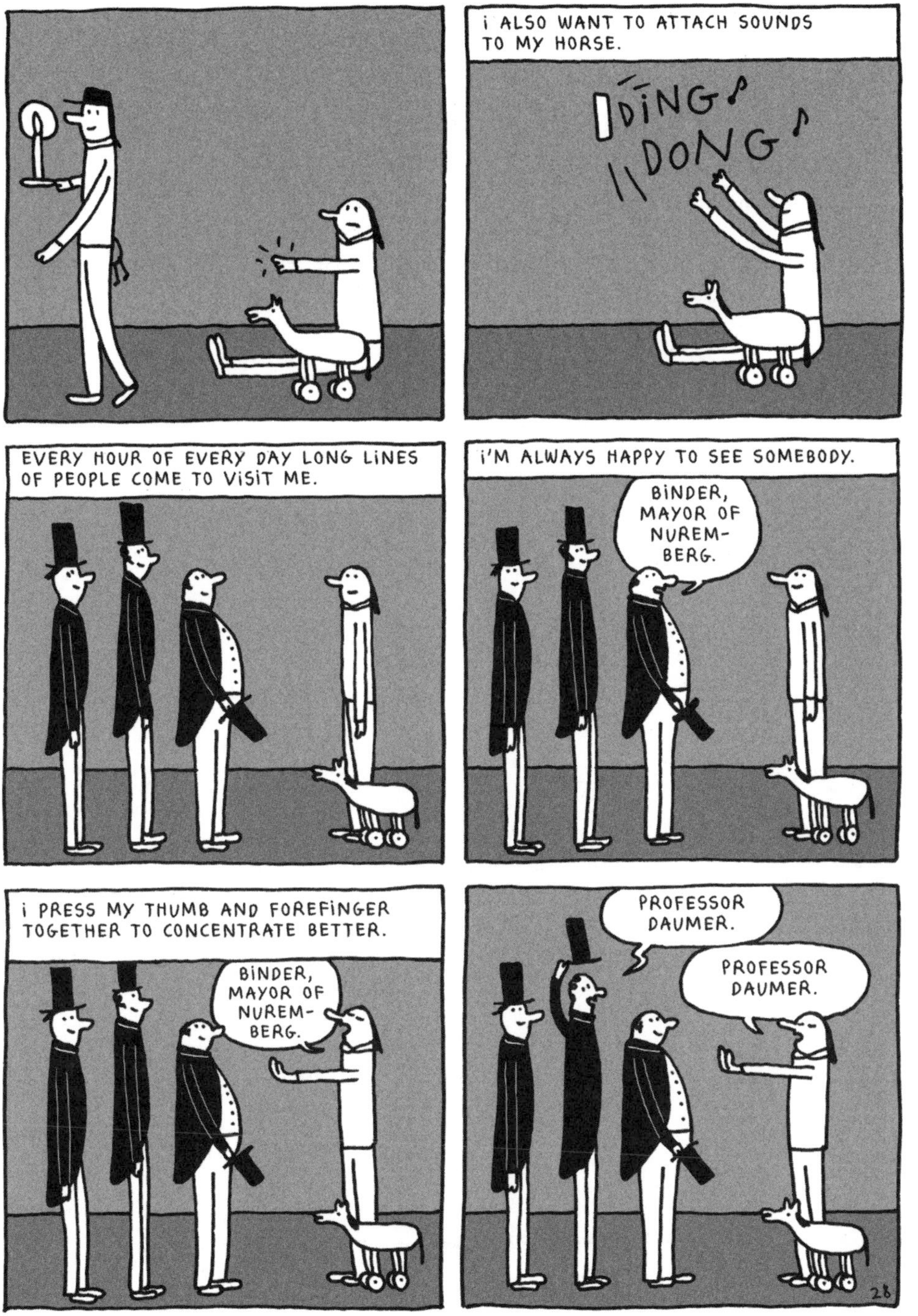

i ALSO WANT TO ATTACH SOUNDS TO MY HORSE.
DiNG
DONG
EVERY HOUR OF EVERY DAY LONG LiNES OF PEOPLE COME TO ViSiT ME.
i'M ALWAYS HAPPY TO SEE SOMEBODY.
BiNDER, MAYOR OF NUREM- BERG.
i PRESS MY THUMB AND FOREFiNGER TOGETHER TO CONCENTRATE BETTER.
BiNDER, MAYOR OF NUREM- BERG.
PROFESSOR DAUMER.
PROFESSOR DAUMER.

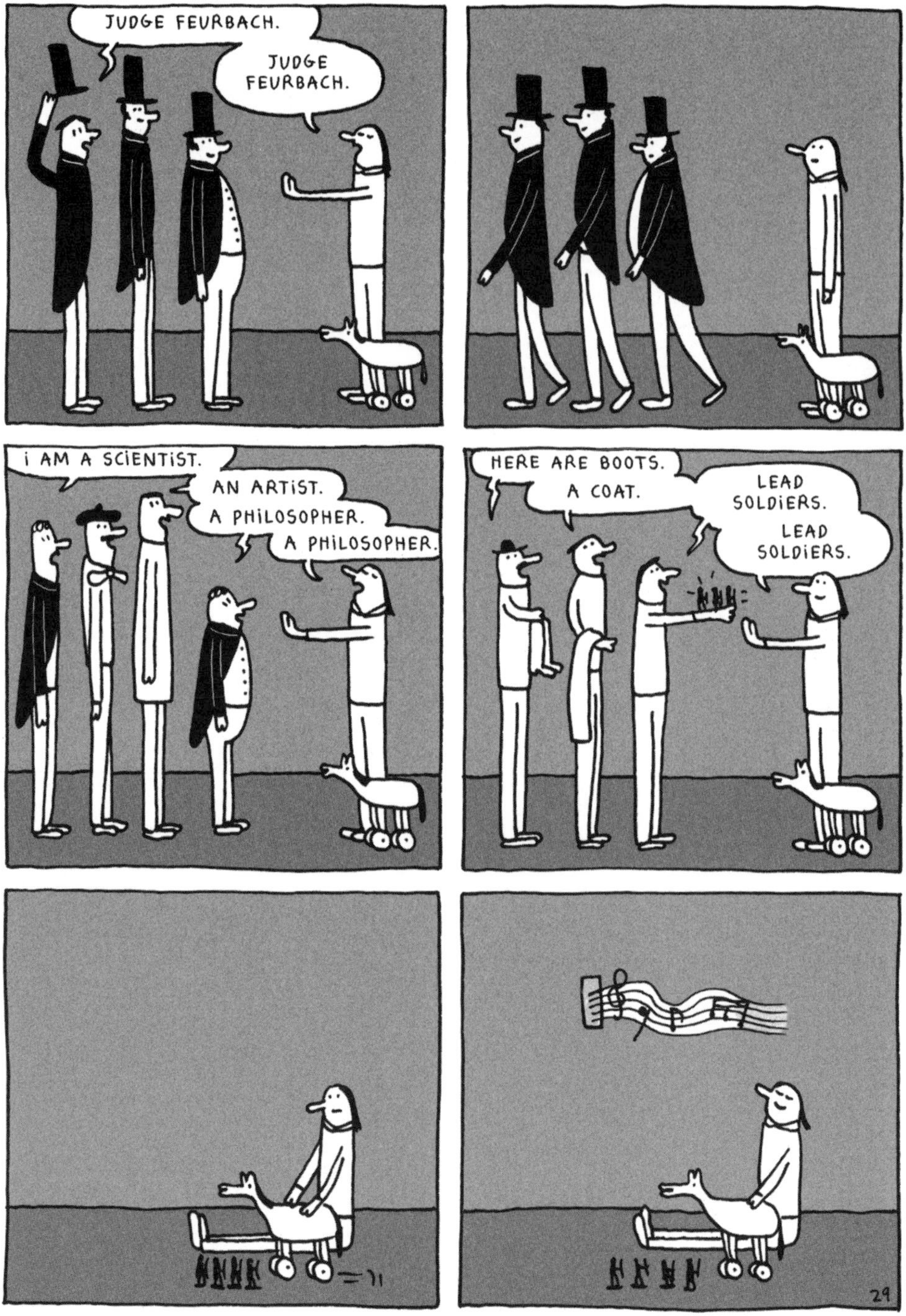
JUDGE FEURBACH.
JUDGE FEURBACH.
I AM A SCIENTIST.
AN ARTIST.
A PHILOSOPHER.
A PHILOSOPHER.
HERE ARE BOOTS.
A COAT.
LEAD SOLDIERS.
LEAD SOLDIERS.

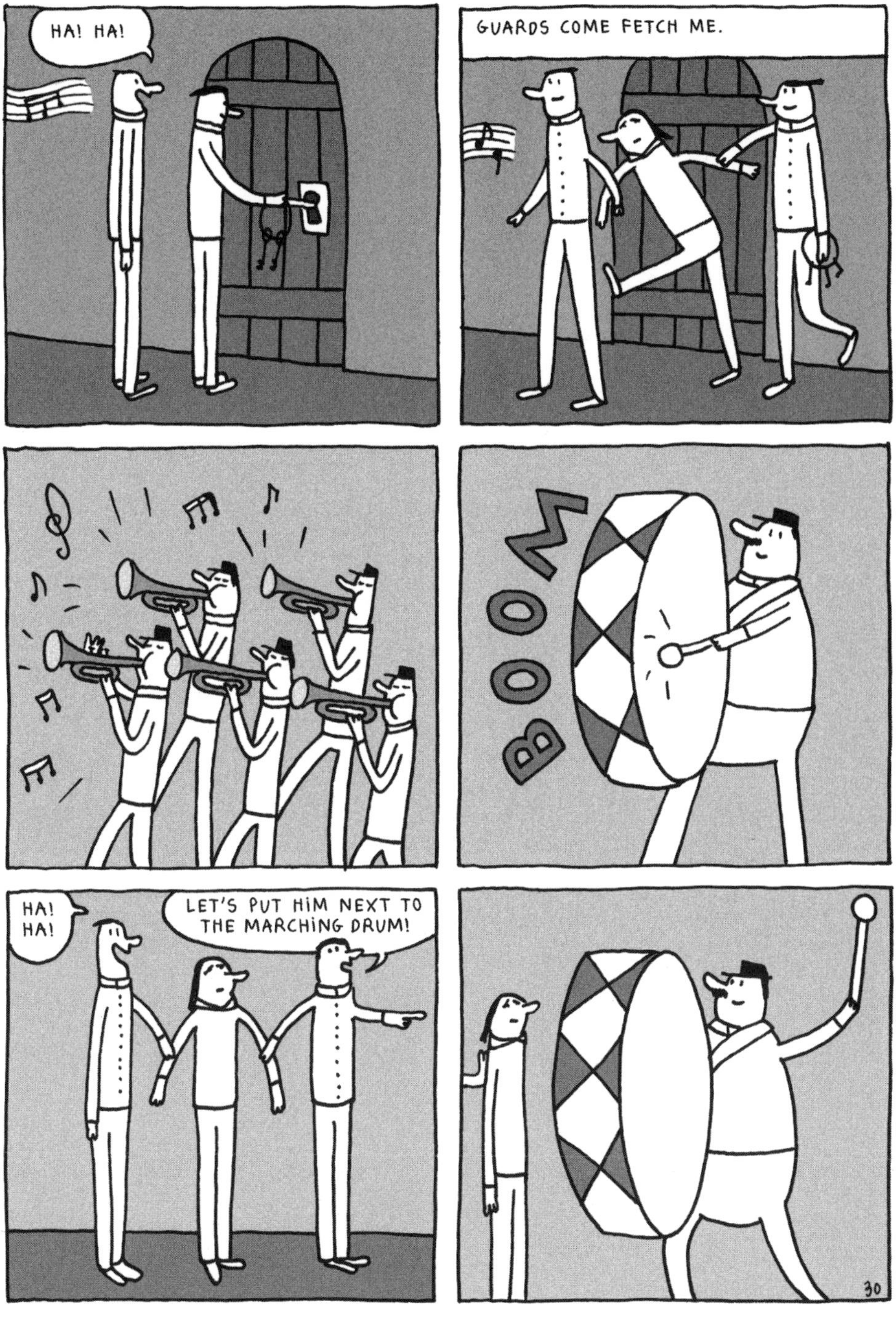
HA! HA!
GUARDS COME FETCH ME.
BOOM
HA! HA!
LET'S PUT HIM NEXT TO THE MARCHING DRUM!

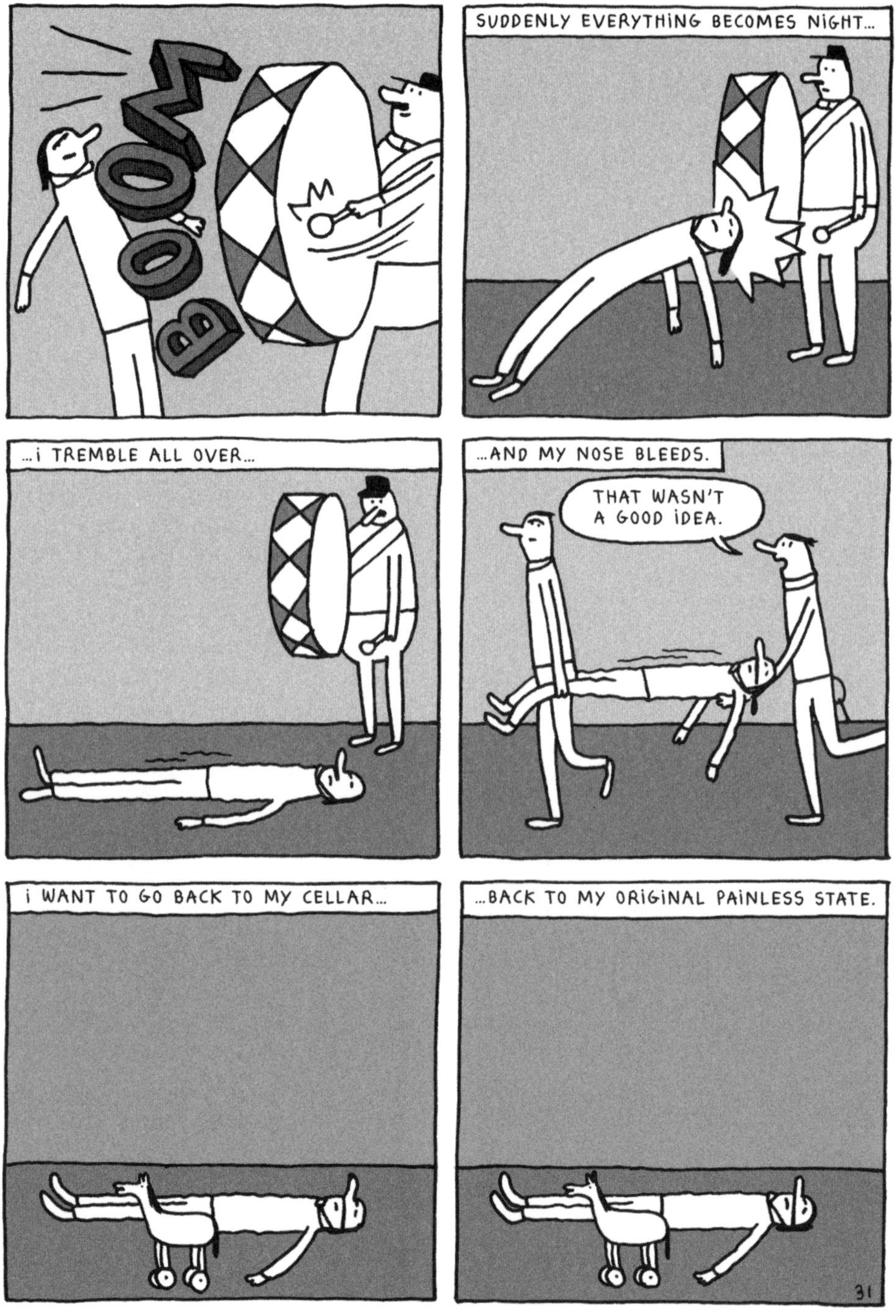
BOOM
SUDDENLY EVERYTHING BECOMES NIGHT...
...I TREMBLE ALL OVER...
...AND MY NOSE BLEEDS.
THAT WASN'T A GOOD IDEA.
I WANT TO GO BACK TO MY CELLAR...
...BACK TO MY ORIGINAL PAINLESS STATE.

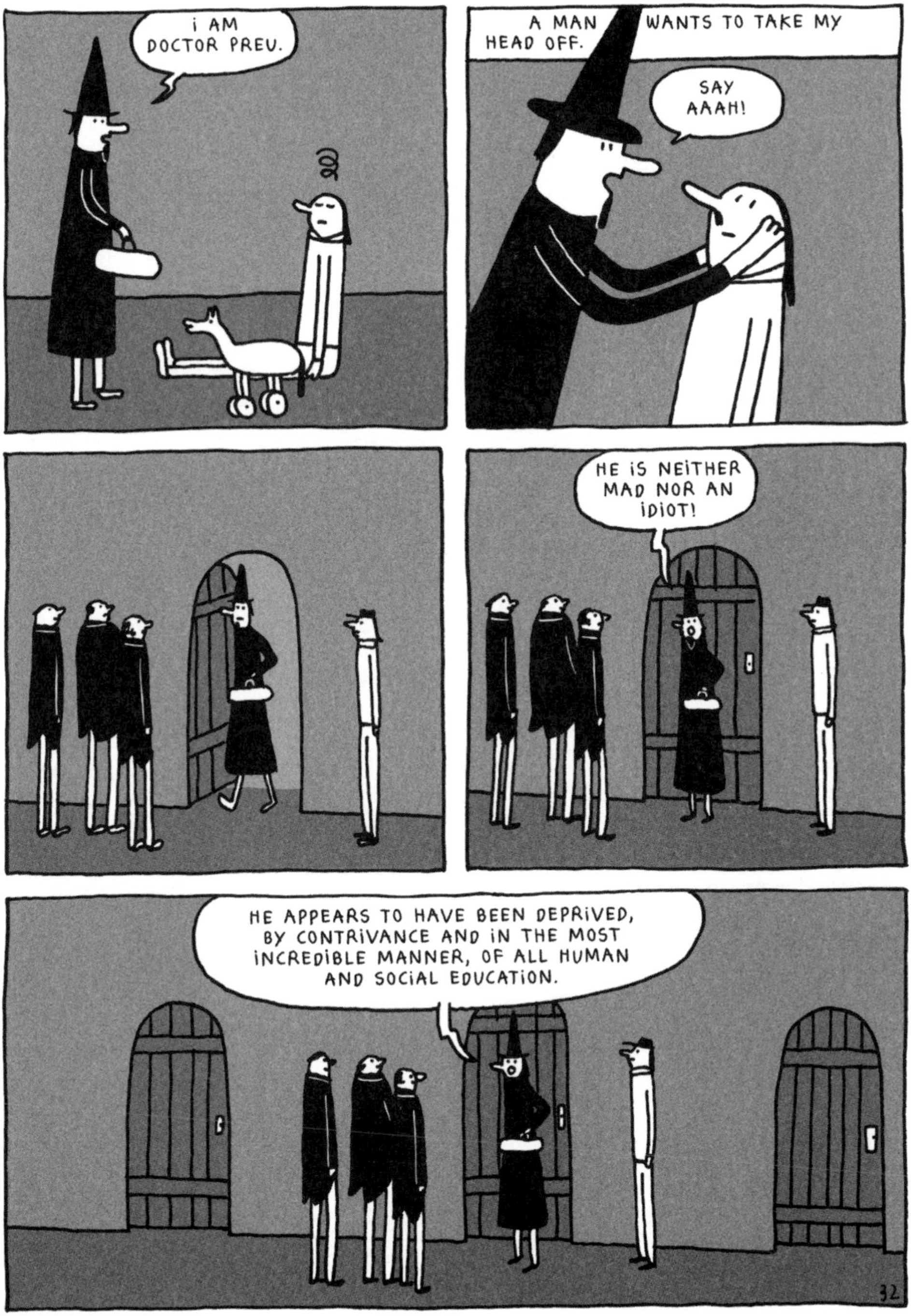
I AM DOCTOR PREU.
A MAN WANTS TO TAKE MY HEAD OFF.
SAY AAAH!
HE IS NEITHER MAD NOR AN IDIOT!
HE APPEARS TO HAVE BEEN DEPRIVED, BY CONTRIVANCE AND IN THE MOST INCREDIBLE MANNER, OF ALL HUMAN AND SOCIAL EDUCATION.
32

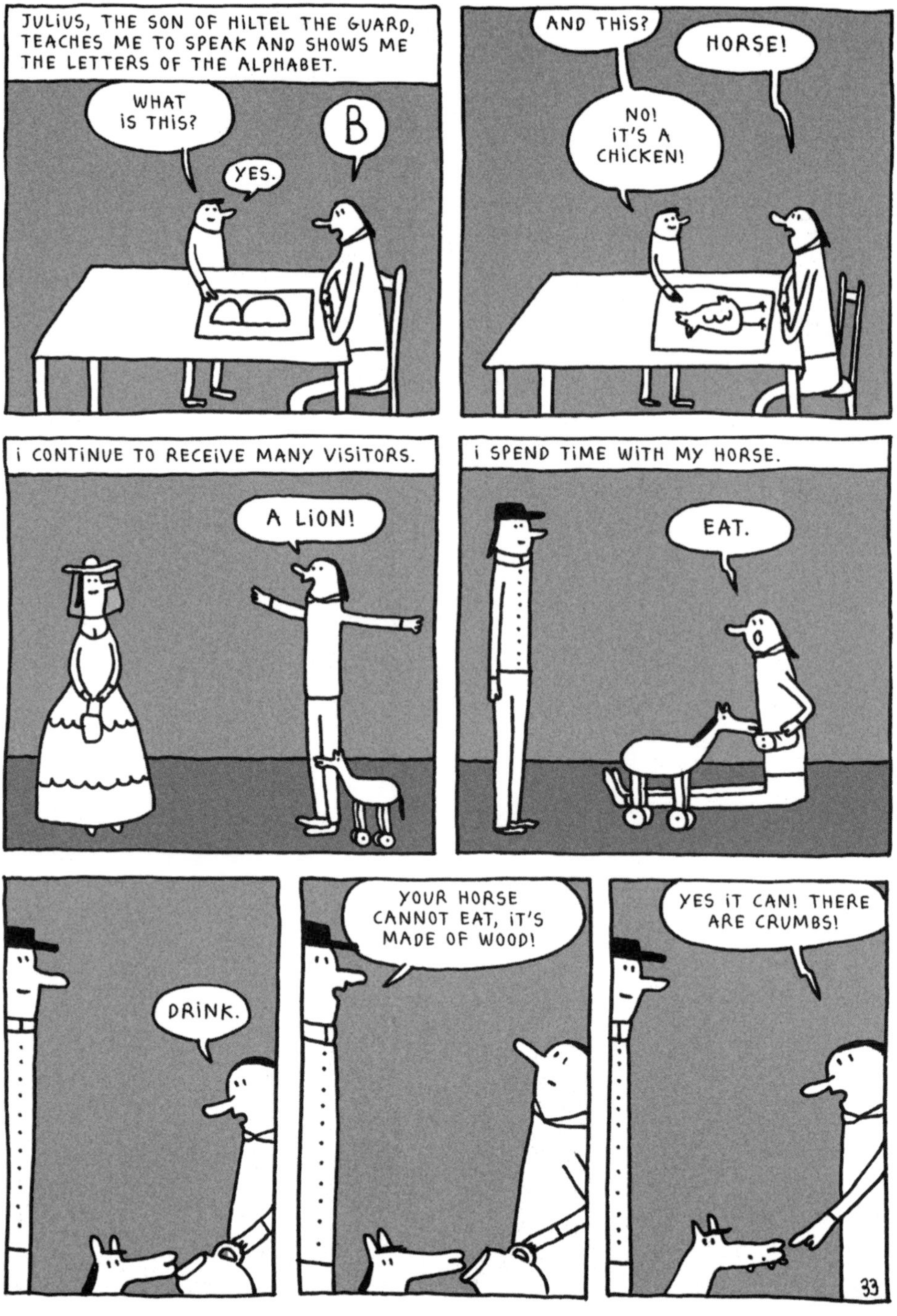
JULIUS, THE SON OF HILTEL THE GUARD, TEACHES ME TO SPEAK AND SHOWS ME THE LETTERS OF THE ALPHABET.
WHAT IS THIS?
B
YES.
AND THIS?
HORSE!
NO! IT'S A CHICKEN!
I CONTINUE TO RECEIVE MANY VISITORS.
A LION!
I SPEND TIME WITH MY HORSE.
EAT.
DRINK.
YOUR HORSE CANNOT EAT, IT'S MADE OF WOOD!
YES IT CAN! THERE ARE CRUMBS!
33

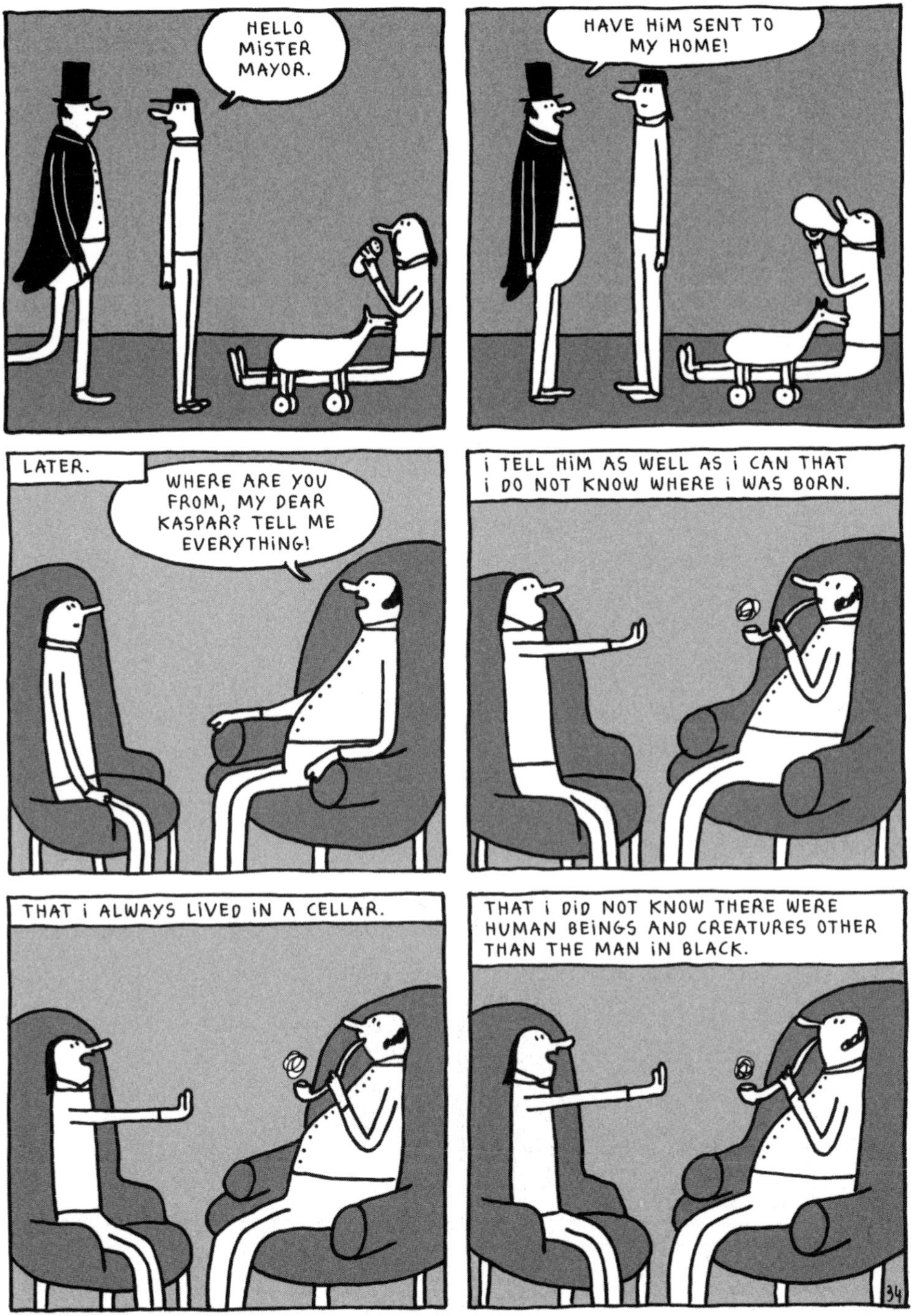
HELLO MISTER MAYOR.
HAVE HIM SENT TO MY HOME!
LATER.
WHERE ARE YOU FROM, MY DEAR KASPAR? TELL ME EVERYTHING!
I TELL HIM AS WELL AS I CAN THAT I DO NOT KNOW WHERE I WAS BORN.
THAT I ALWAYS LIVED IN A CELLAR.
THAT I DID NOT KNOW THERE WERE HUMAN BEINGS AND CREATURES OTHER THAN THE MAN IN BLACK.

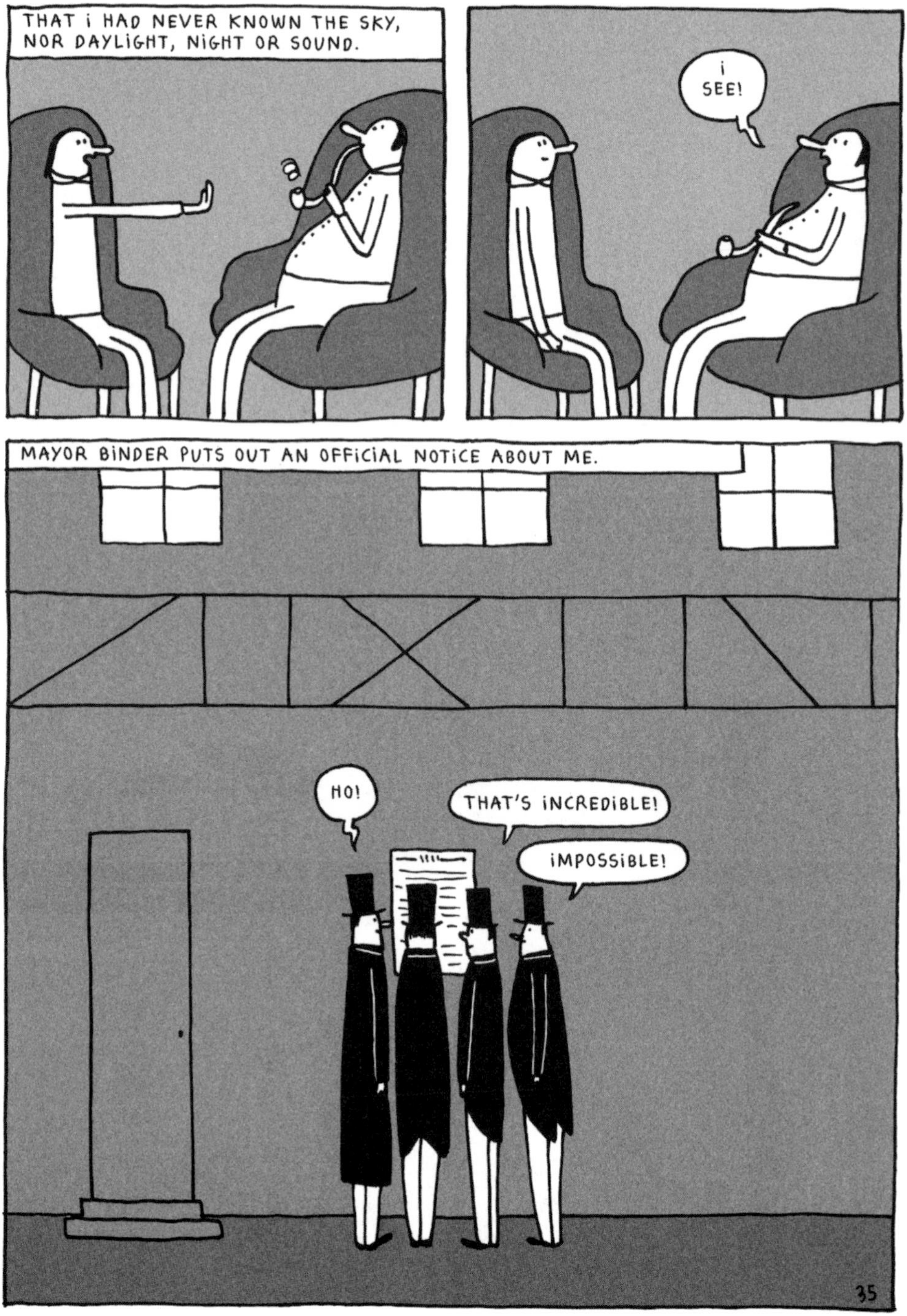
THAT i HAD NEVER KNOWN THE SKY, NOR DAYLIGHT, NIGHT OR SOUND.
i SEE!
MAYOR BINDER PUTS OUT AN OFFICIAL NOTICE ABOUT ME.
HO!
THAT'S iNCREDIBLE!
iMPOSSIBLE!

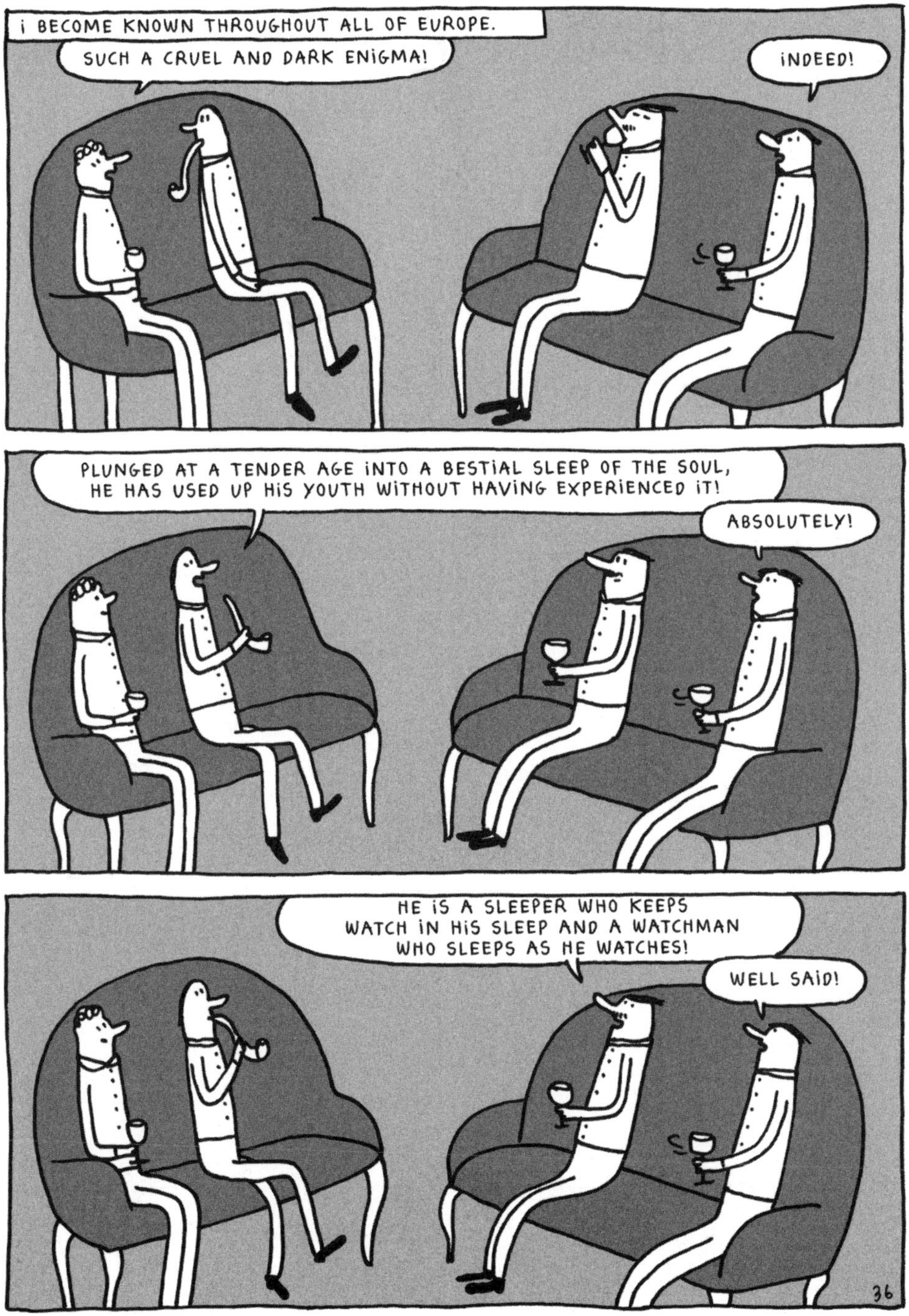
I BECOME KNOWN THROUGHOUT ALL OF EUROPE.
SUCH A CRUEL AND DARK ENIGMA!
INDEED!
PLUNGED AT A TENDER AGE INTO A BESTIAL SLEEP OF THE SOUL, HE HAS USED UP HIS YOUTH WITHOUT HAVING EXPERIENCED IT!
ABSOLUTELY!
HE IS A SLEEPER WHO KEEPS WATCH IN HIS SLEEP AND A WATCHMAN WHO SLEEPS AS HE WATCHES!
WELL SAID!
36

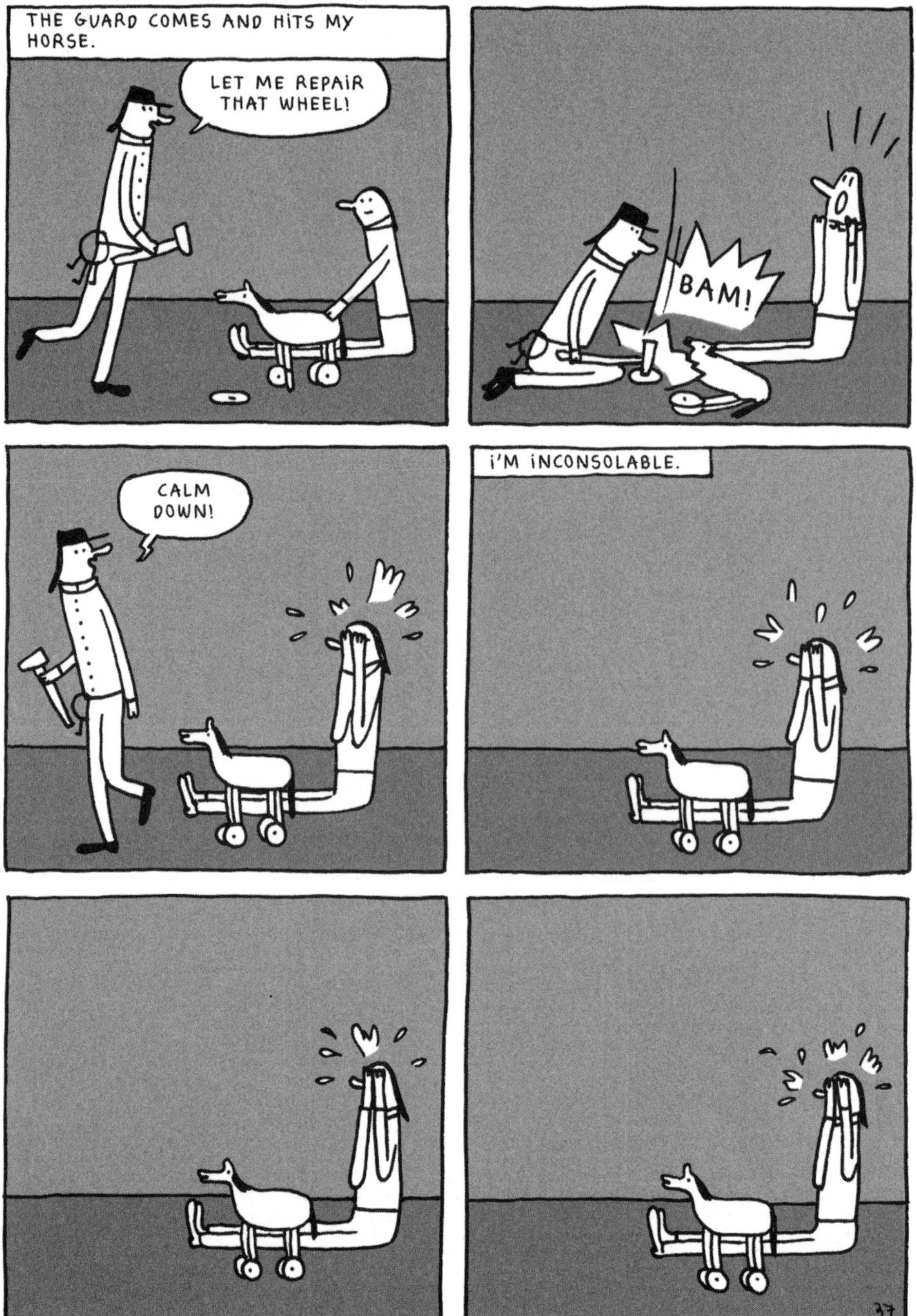

THE GUARD COMES AND HITS MY HORSE.
LET ME REPAIR THAT WHEEL!
BAM!
CALM DOWN!
I'M INCONSOLABLE.

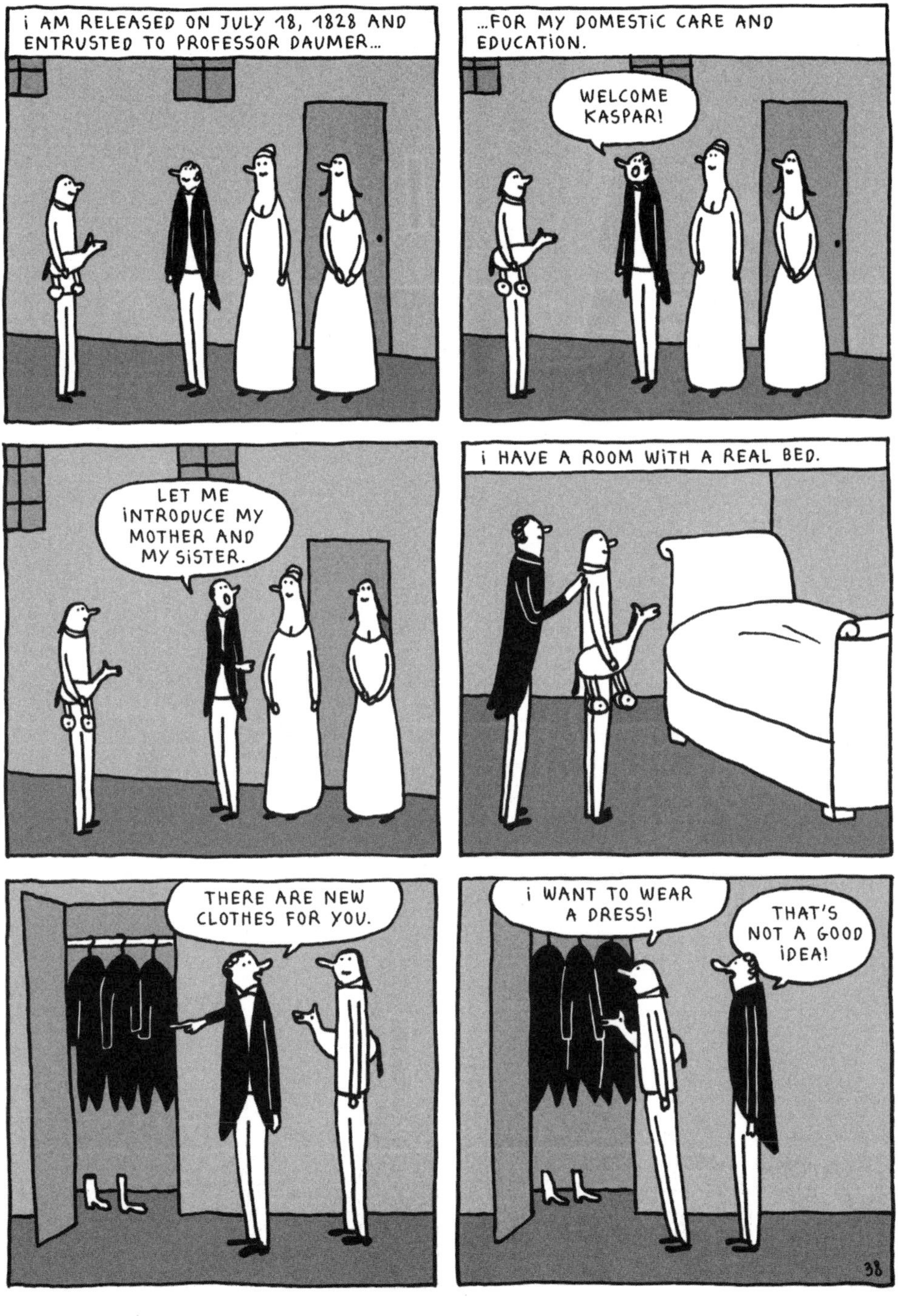
i AM RELEASED ON JULY 18, 1828 AND ENTRUSTED TO PROFESSOR DAUMER...
...FOR MY DOMESTiC CARE AND EDUCATiON.
WELCOME KASPAR!
LET ME iNTRODUCE MY MOTHER AND MY SiSTER.
i HAVE A ROOM WiTH A REAL BED.
THERE ARE NEW CLOTHES FOR YOU.
i WANT TO WEAR A DRESS!
THAT'S NOT A GOOD iDEA!
38

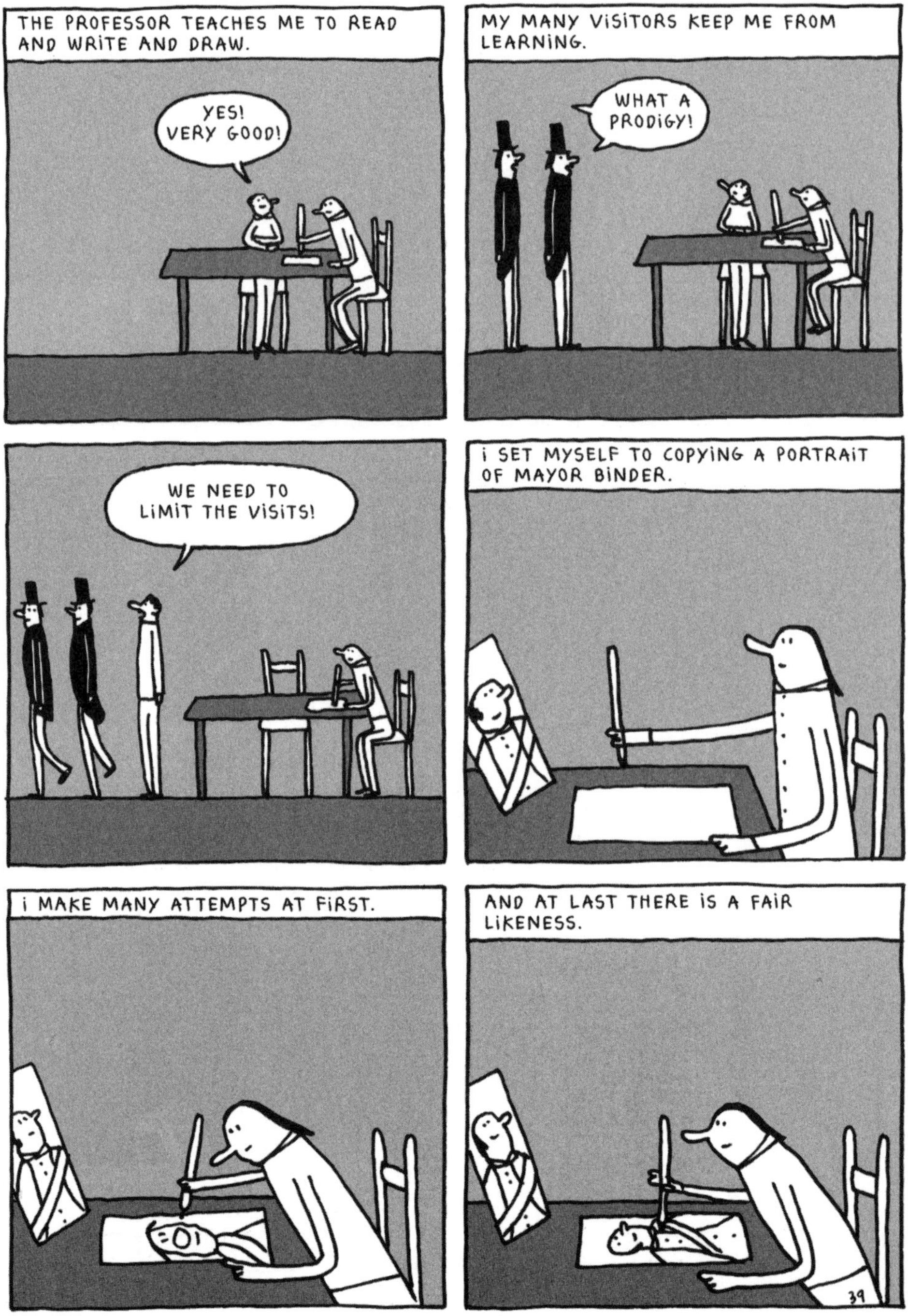
THE PROFESSOR TEACHES ME TO READ AND WRITE AND DRAW.
YES! VERY GOOD!
MY MANY VISITORS KEEP ME FROM LEARNING.
WHAT A PRODIGY!
WE NEED TO LIMIT THE VISITS!
I SET MYSELF TO COPYING A PORTRAIT OF MAYOR BINDER.
I MAKE MANY ATTEMPTS AT FIRST.
AND AT LAST THERE IS A FAIR LIKENESS.

I FEEL HAPPY. I WRITE MY FIRST POEM.

TODAY I WELCOME MY FIRST YEAR
WITH LOVING HEART AND GRATEFUL CHEER.
THOUGH I HAVE BEEN OPPRESSED BY CARES,
MY HEART NOW COMFORTABLY WEARS
THE NEWFOUND HAPPINESS IT BEARS.
AND HERE IN MY FIRST YEAR I FACE
SO MUCH TO DO, AT SUCH A PACE:
TO WRITE AND PAINT LIFE'S WONDERS,
TO CALCULATE WITH NUMBERS.
GOD BIDS ME WATCH THE WORLD AT HAND
AND READ MY BOOKS, AND UNDERSTAND,
AND TEND MY LITTLE PATCH OF LAND.
WHILE I AM YOUNG, GOD GIVES ME STRENGTH
TO QUESTION WISE MEN AT GREAT LENGTH.
AND SO I MUST MAKE PREPARATION
TO DAILY SEEK MY EDUCATION.
THE GOAL IS FAR, EACH STEP IS SMALL
BUT I WILL REACH IT AFTER ALL.

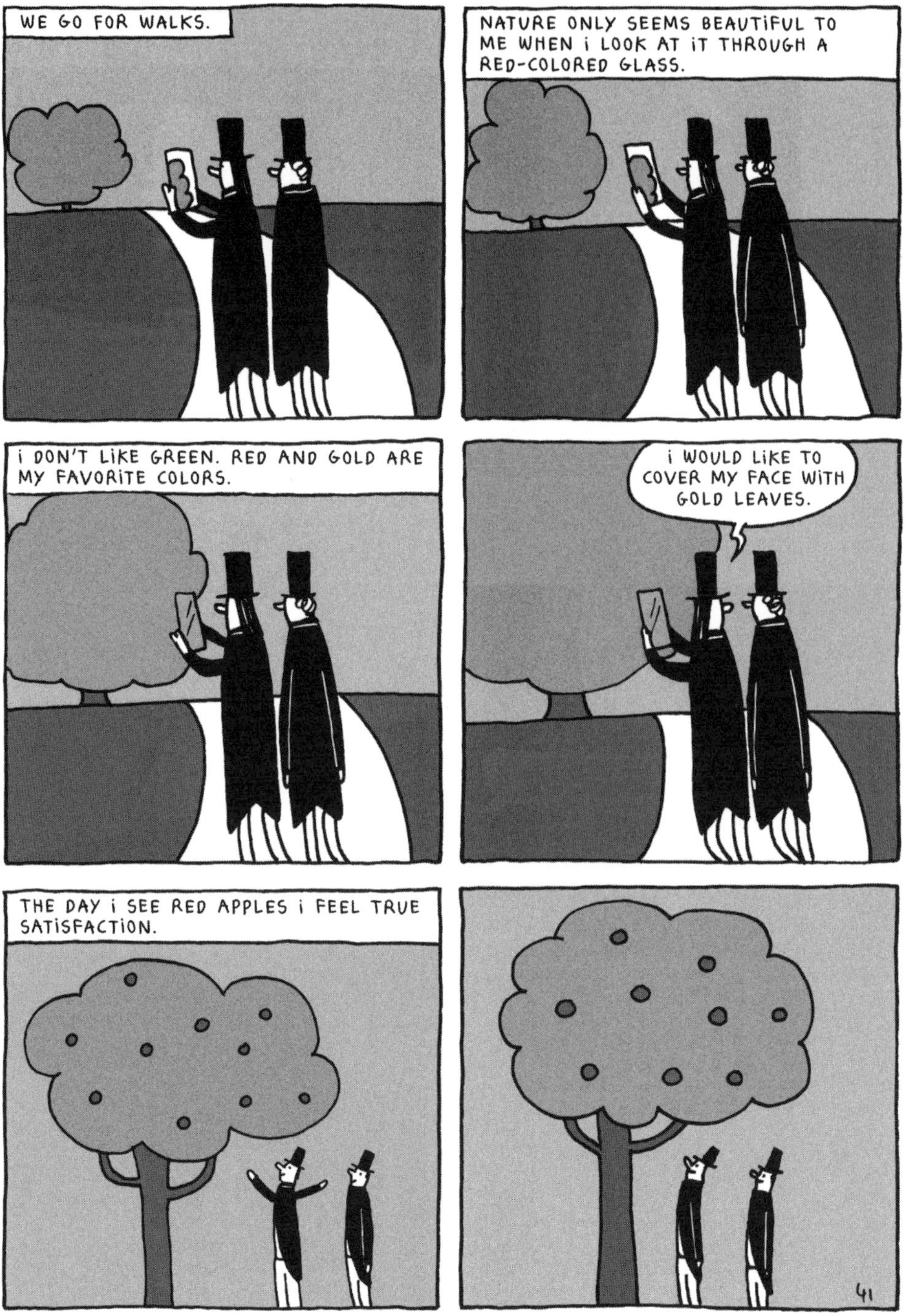
WE GO FOR WALKS.
NATURE ONLY SEEMS BEAUTIFUL TO ME WHEN i LOOK AT iT THROUGH A RED-COLORED GLASS.
i DON'T LiKE GREEN. RED AND GOLD ARE MY FAVORiTE COLORS.
i WOULD LiKE TO COVER MY FACE WiTH GOLD LEAVES.
THE DAY i SEE RED APPLES i FEEL TRUE SATiSFACTiON.
41

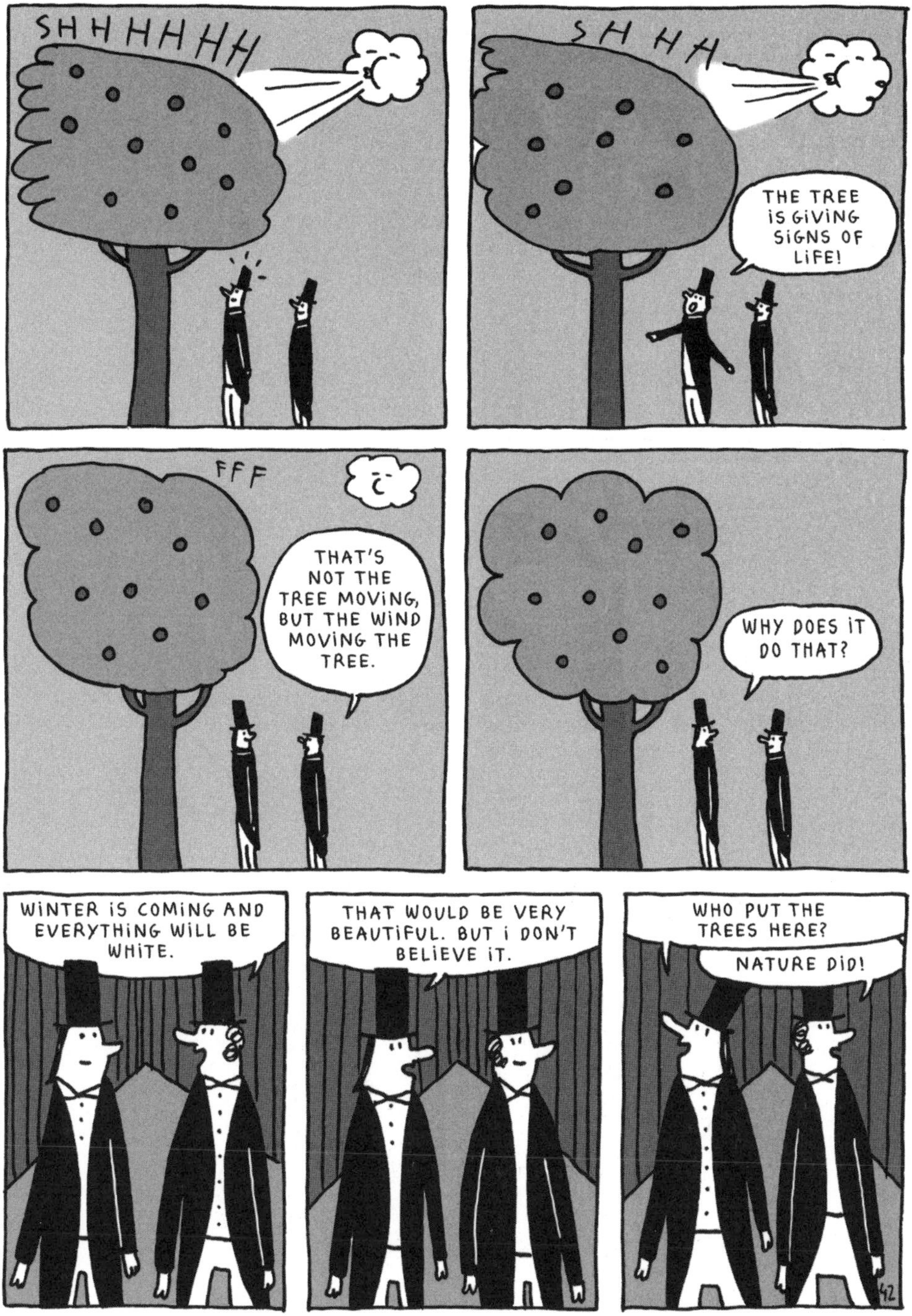
SHHHHHH
SHHH
THE TREE IS GIVING SIGNS OF LIFE!
FFF
THAT'S NOT THE TREE MOVING, BUT THE WIND MOVING THE TREE.
WHY DOES IT DO THAT?
WINTER IS COMING AND EVERYTHING WILL BE WHITE.
THAT WOULD BE VERY BEAUTIFUL. BUT I DON'T BELIEVE IT.
WHO PUT THE TREES HERE?
NATURE DID!
42

THE PROFESSOR SHOWS ME HOW TO GARDEN.
MAKE A HOLE WITH YOUR FINGER...
...AND DROP IN A BEAN SEED.
THE SEEDS WILL SPROUT AND GROW.
A FEW DAYS LATER.
OH!
I SOW MY NAME WITH GARDEN CRESS SEEDS.
KASPA

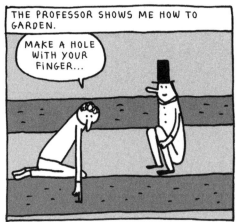

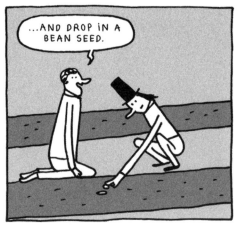

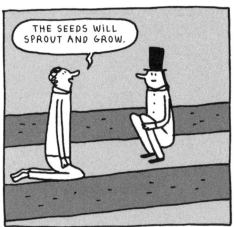

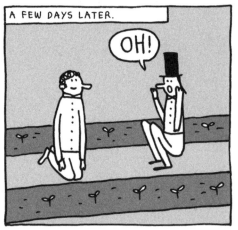

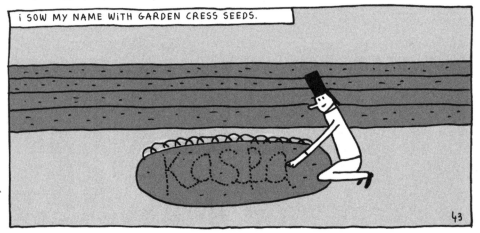

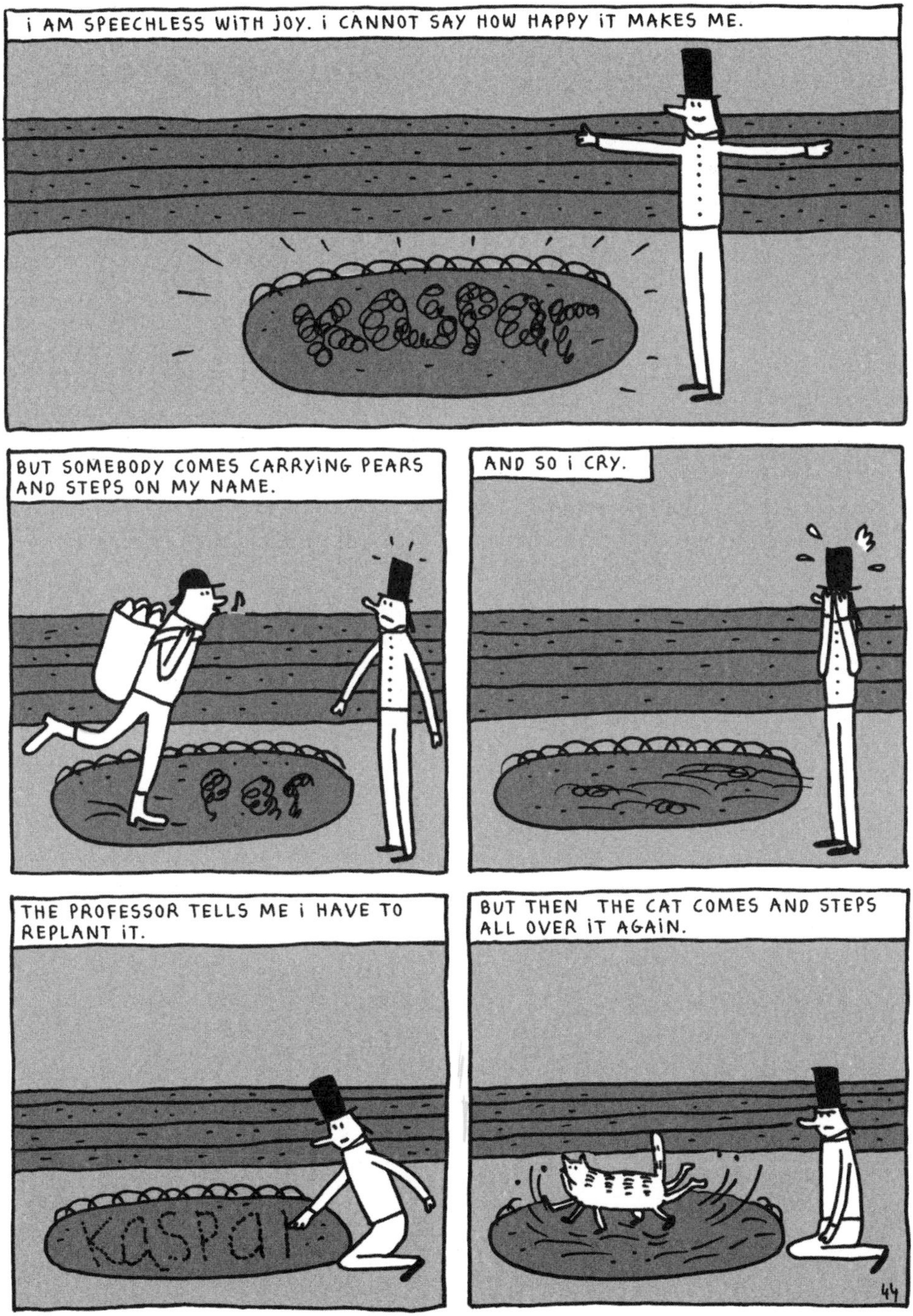
i AM SPEECHLESS WiTH JOY. i CANNOT SAY HOW HAPPY iT MAKES ME.
BUT SOMEBODY COMES CARRYiNG PEARS AND STEPS ON MY NAME.
AND SO i CRY.
THE PROFESSOR TELLS ME i HAVE TO REPLANT iT.
BUT THEN THE CAT COMES AND STEPS ALL OVER iT AGAiN.

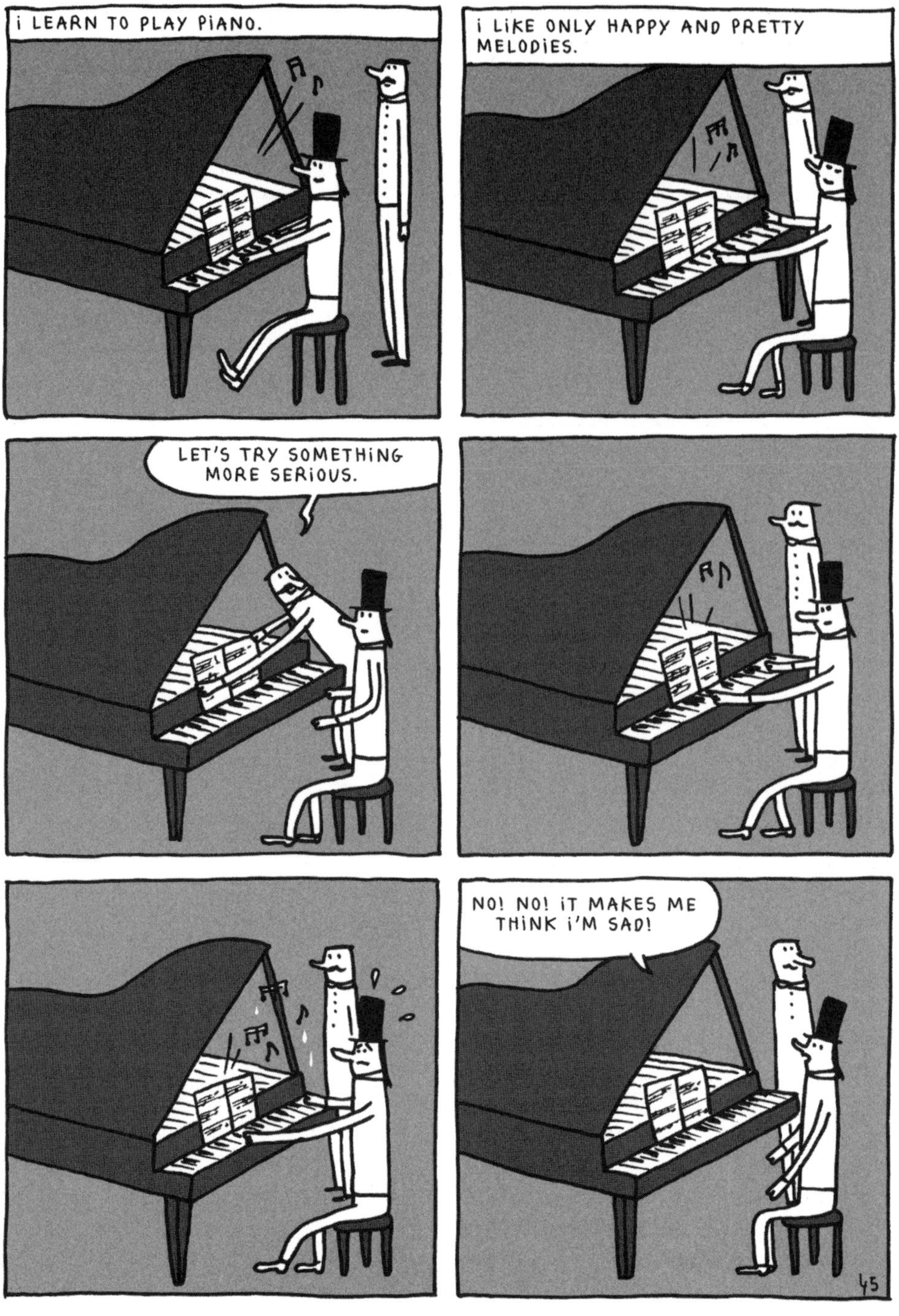

i LEARN TO PLAY PiANO.
i LiKE ONLY HAPPY AND PRETTY MELODiES.
LET'S TRY SOMETHiNG MORE SERiOUS.
NO! NO! iT MAKES ME THiNK i'M SAD!

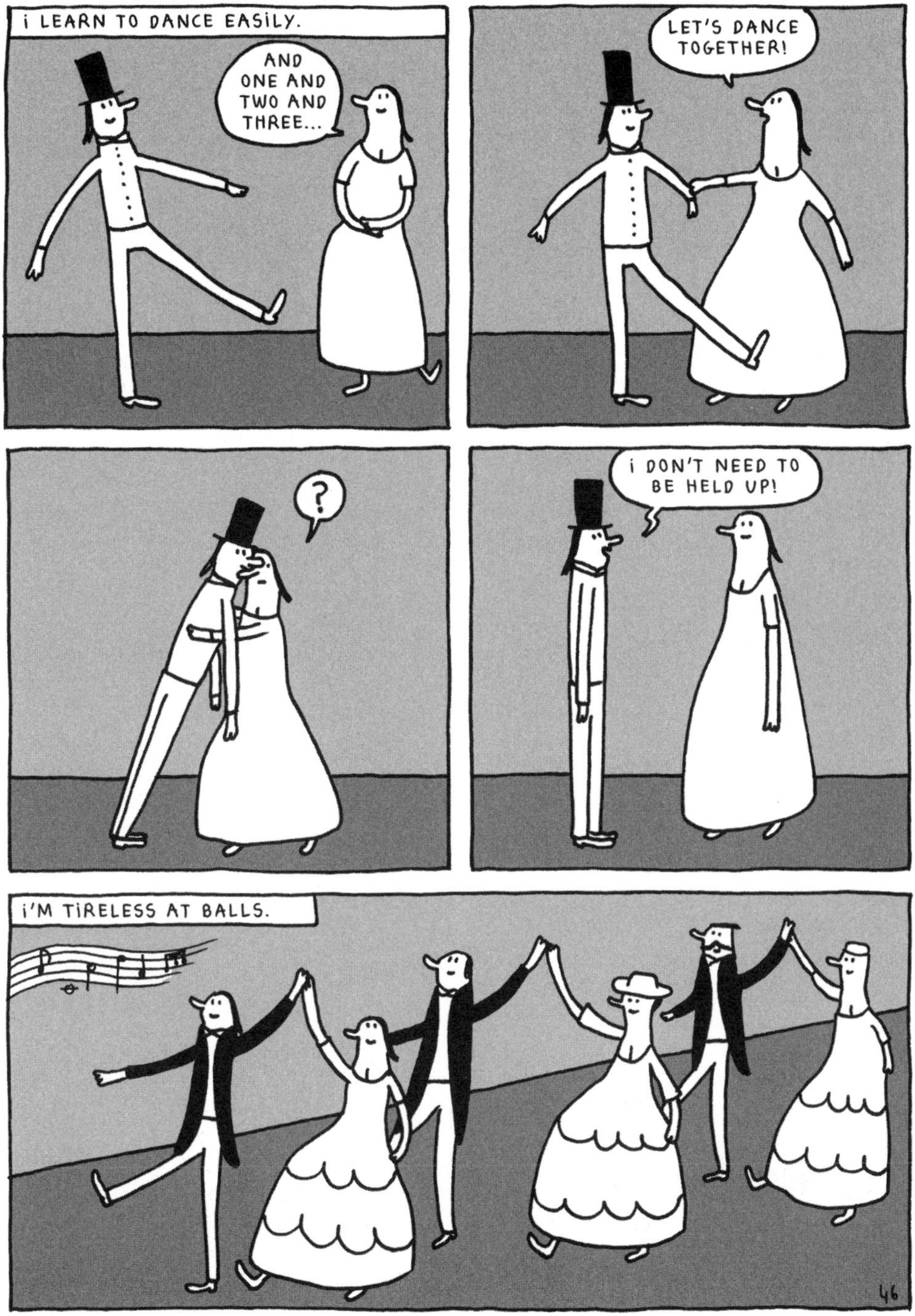
i LEARN TO DANCE EASiLY.
AND ONE AND TWO AND THREE...
LET'S DANCE TOGETHER!
?
i DON'T NEED TO BE HELD UP!
i'M TIRELESS AT BALLS.
46

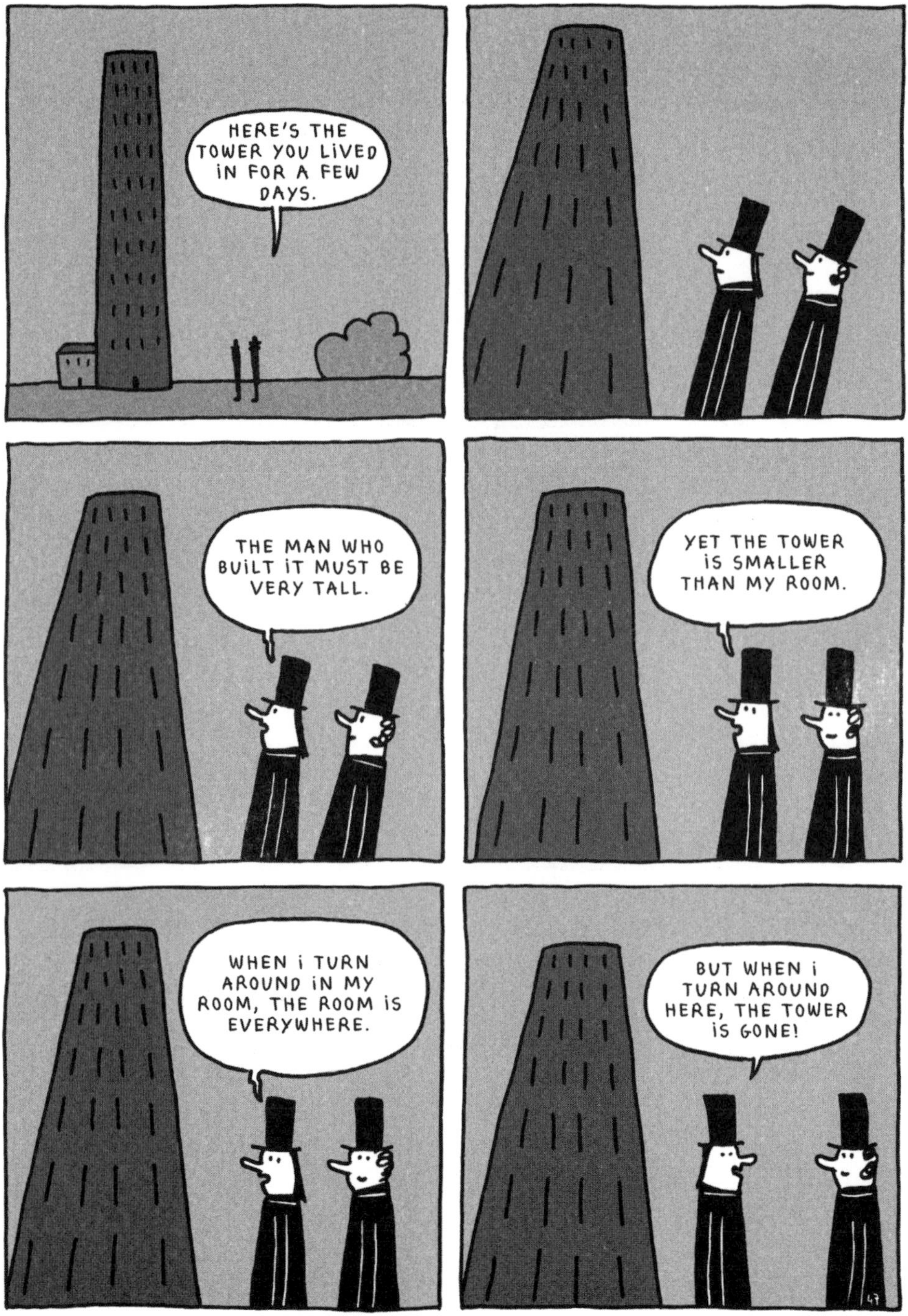
HERE'S THE TOWER YOU LIVED IN FOR A FEW DAYS.
THE MAN WHO BUILT IT MUST BE VERY TALL.
YET THE TOWER IS SMALLER THAN MY ROOM.
WHEN I TURN AROUND IN MY ROOM, THE ROOM IS EVERYWHERE.
BUT WHEN I TURN AROUND HERE, THE TOWER IS GONE!
47

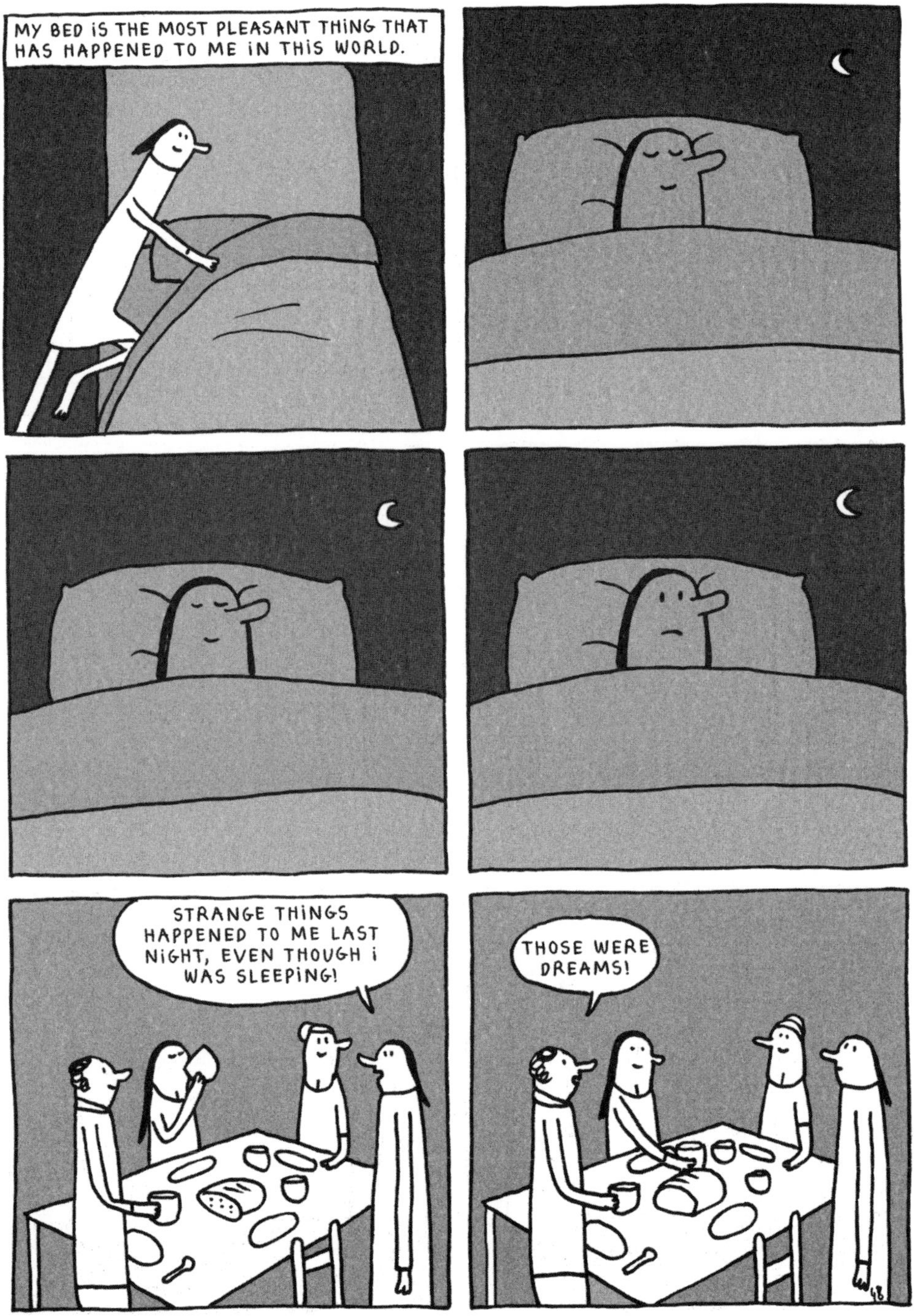
MY BED IS THE MOST PLEASANT THING THAT HAS HAPPENED TO ME IN THIS WORLD.
STRANGE THINGS HAPPENED TO ME LAST NIGHT, EVEN THOUGH I WAS SLEEPING!
THOSE WERE DREAMS!

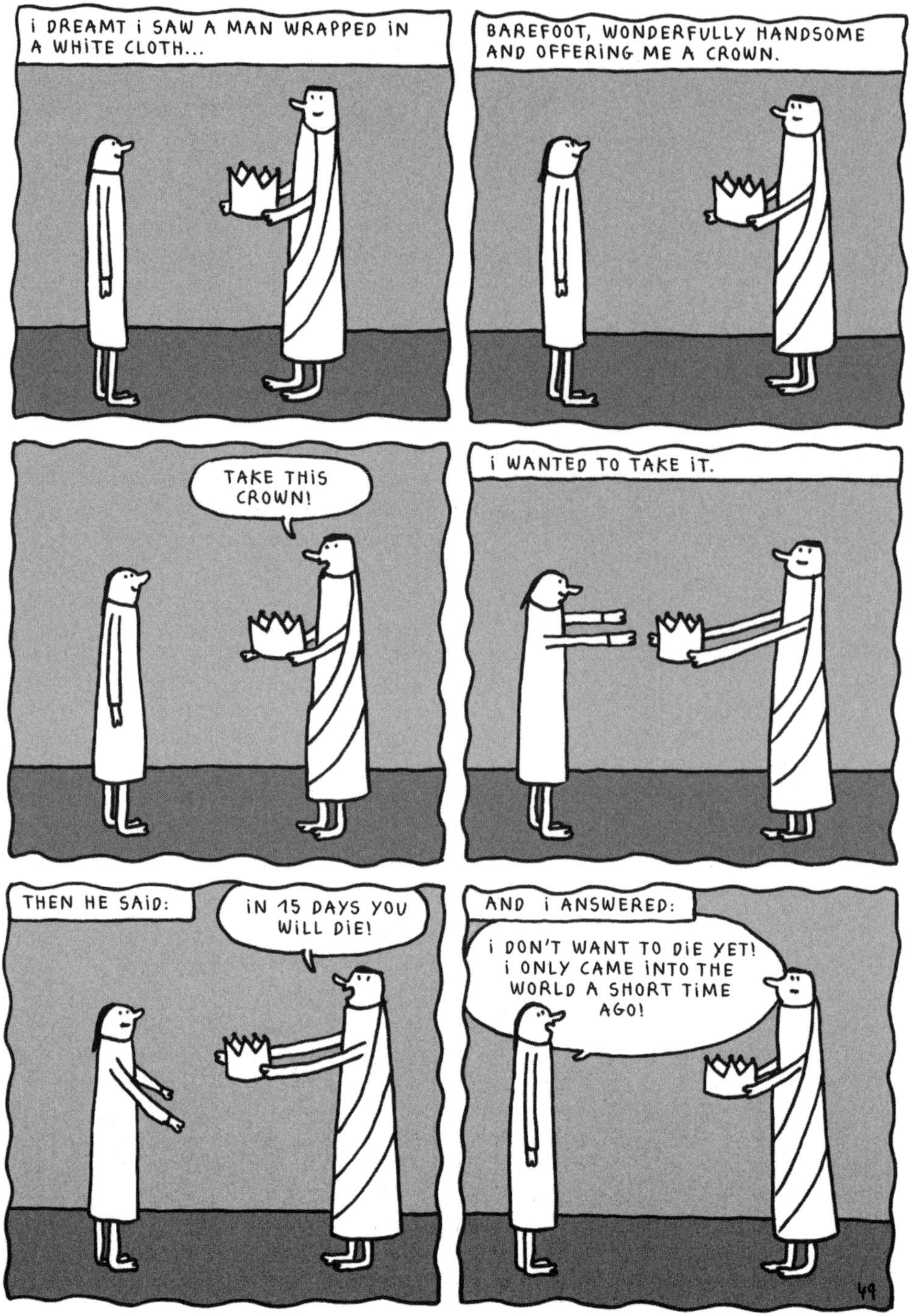
i DREAMT i SAW A MAN WRAPPED iN A WHiTE CLOTH...
BAREFOOT, WONDERFULLY HANDSOME AND OFFERiNG ME A CROWN.
TAKE THiS CROWN!
i WANTED TO TAKE iT.
THEN HE SAiD:
iN 15 DAYS YOU WiLL DiE!
AND i ANSWERED:
i DON'T WANT TO DiE YET! i ONLY CAME iNTO THE WORLD A SHORT TiME AGO!

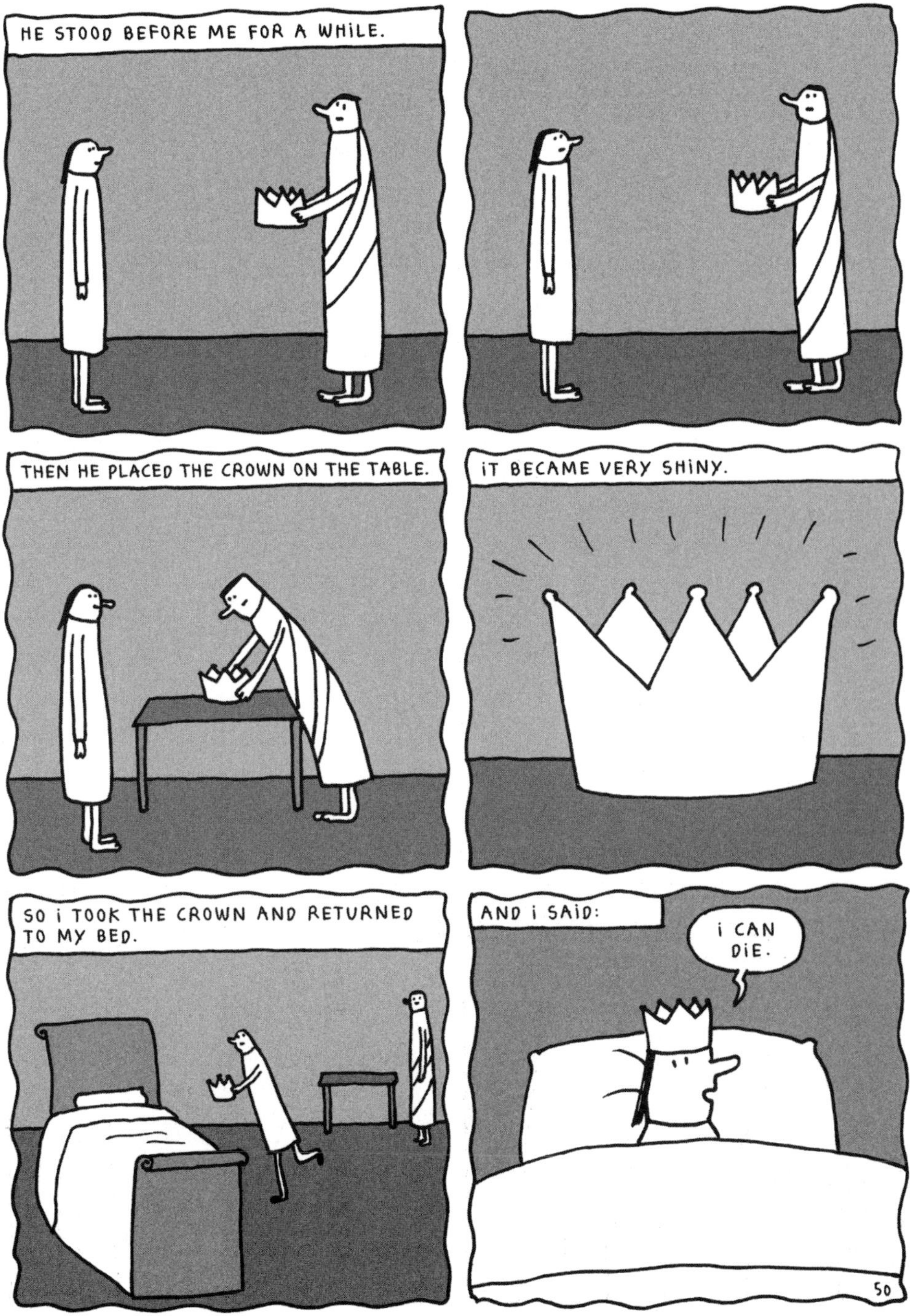
HE STOOD BEFORE ME FOR A WHILE.
THEN HE PLACED THE CROWN ON THE TABLE.
IT BECAME VERY SHINY.
SO I TOOK THE CROWN AND RETURNED TO MY BED.
AND I SAID:
I CAN DIE.

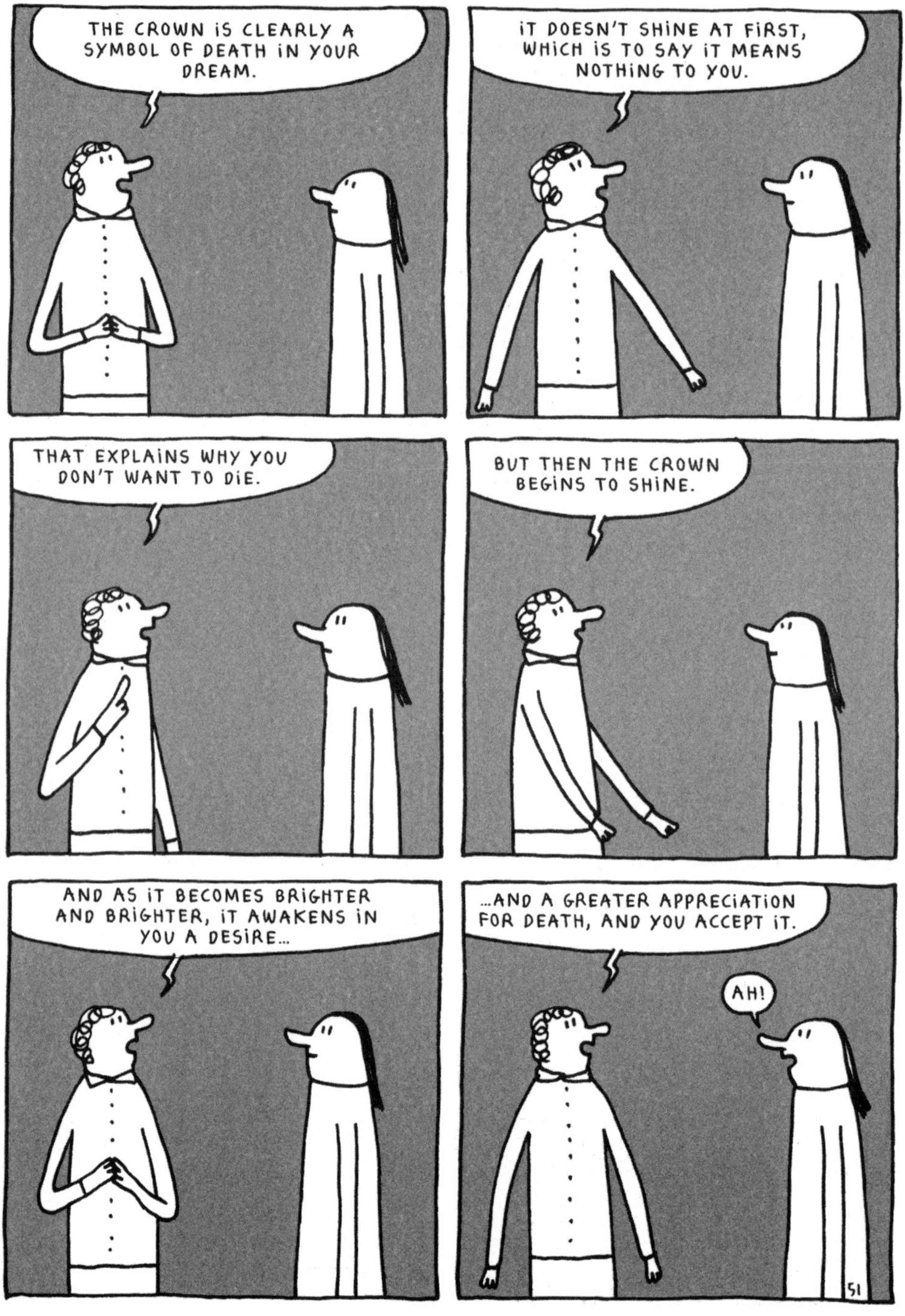
THE CROWN IS CLEARLY A SYMBOL OF DEATH IN YOUR DREAM.
IT DOESN'T SHINE AT FIRST, WHICH IS TO SAY IT MEANS NOTHING TO YOU.
THAT EXPLAINS WHY YOU DON'T WANT TO DIE.
BUT THEN THE CROWN BEGINS TO SHINE.
AND AS IT BECOMES BRIGHTER AND BRIGHTER, IT AWAKENS IN YOU A DESIRE...
...AND A GREATER APPRECIATION FOR DEATH, AND YOU ACCEPT IT.
AH!
51

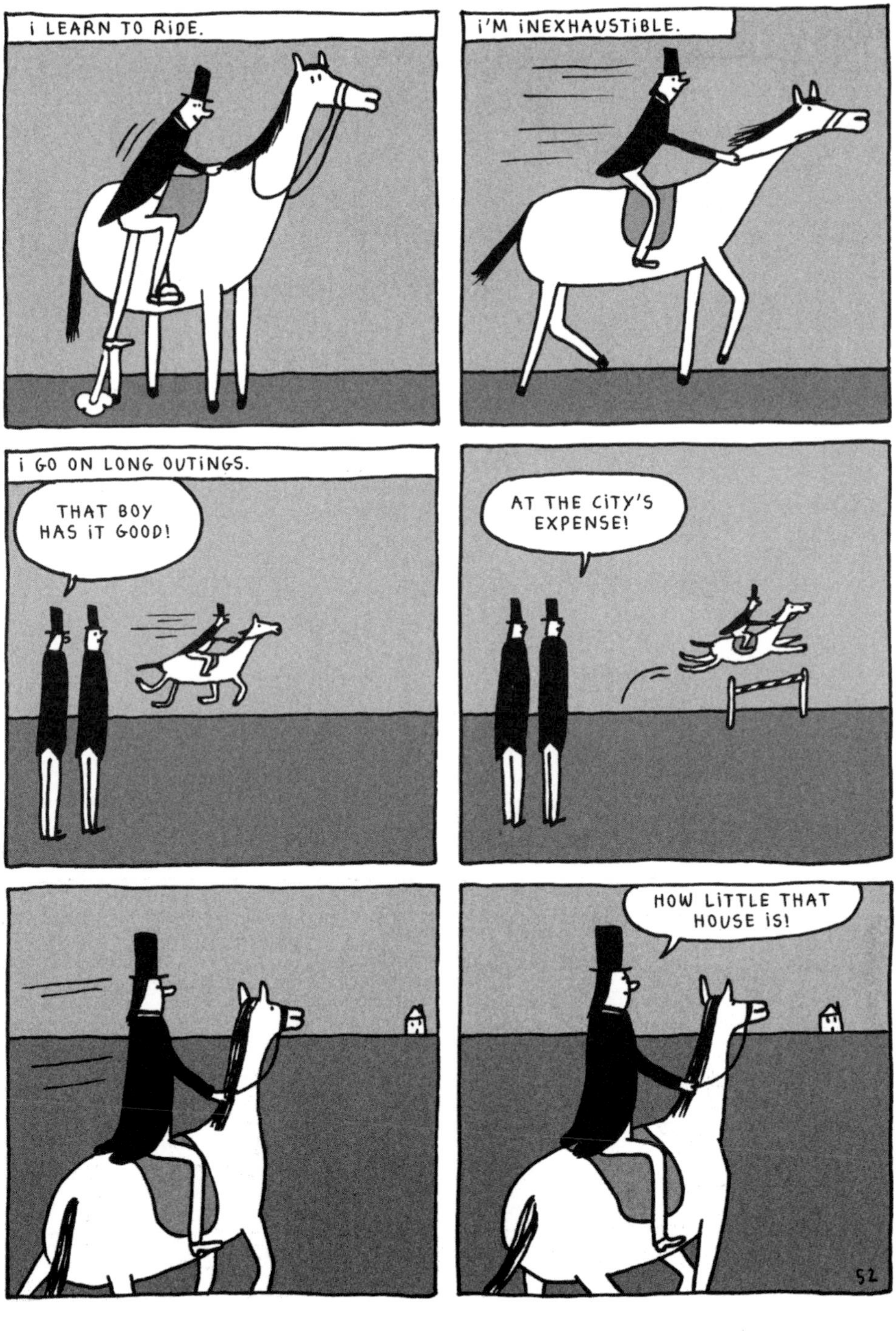
I LEARN TO RIDE.
I'M INEXHAUSTIBLE.
I GO ON LONG OUTINGS.
THAT BOY HAS IT GOOD!
AT THE CITY'S EXPENSE!
HOW LITTLE THAT HOUSE IS!

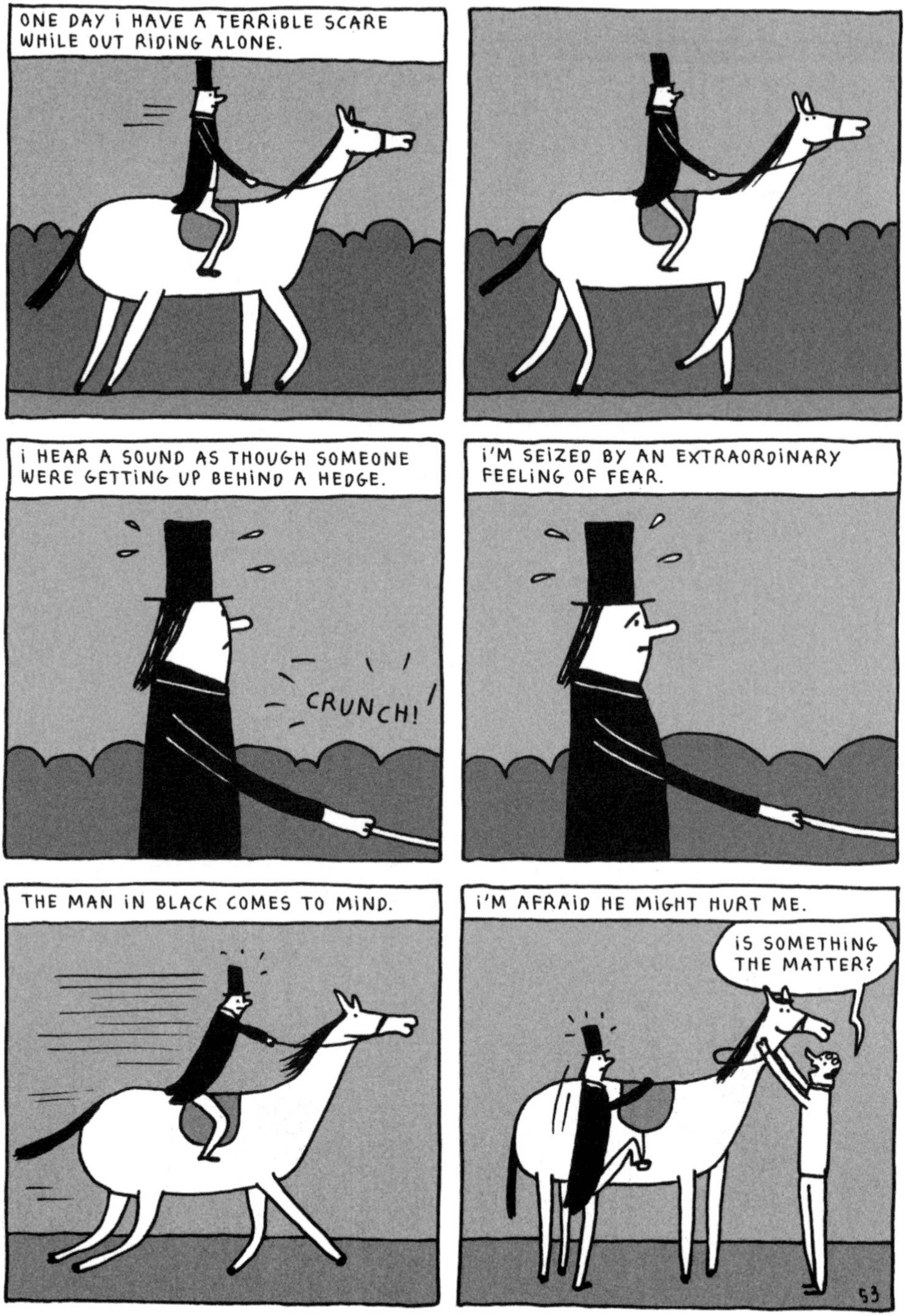
ONE DAY i HAVE A TERRIBLE SCARE WHILE OUT RIDING ALONE.
i HEAR A SOUND AS THOUGH SOMEONE WERE GETTING UP BEHIND A HEDGE.
CRUNCH!
i'M SEIZED BY AN EXTRAORDINARY FEELING OF FEAR.
THE MAN iN BLACK COMES TO MIND.
i'M AFRAID HE MIGHT HURT ME.
iS SOMETHING THE MATTER?

i BECOME INTERESTED IN MY APPEARANCE AND CURL MY HAIR.

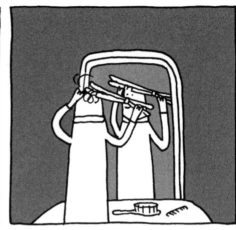

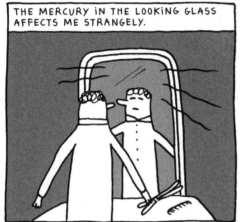

THE MERCURY IN THE LOOKING GLASS AFFECTS ME STRANGELY.

STORMS MAKE ME TREMBLE AND SHAKE.

LiGHTNiNG CAUSES NEEDLE PRiCKS iN MY EYES.

WHEN i SHAKE A PERSON'S HAND i FEEL A SHiVER OF COLD, EXCEPT WITH OLD PEOPLE.

GOOD NiGHT KASPAR

BRRRR

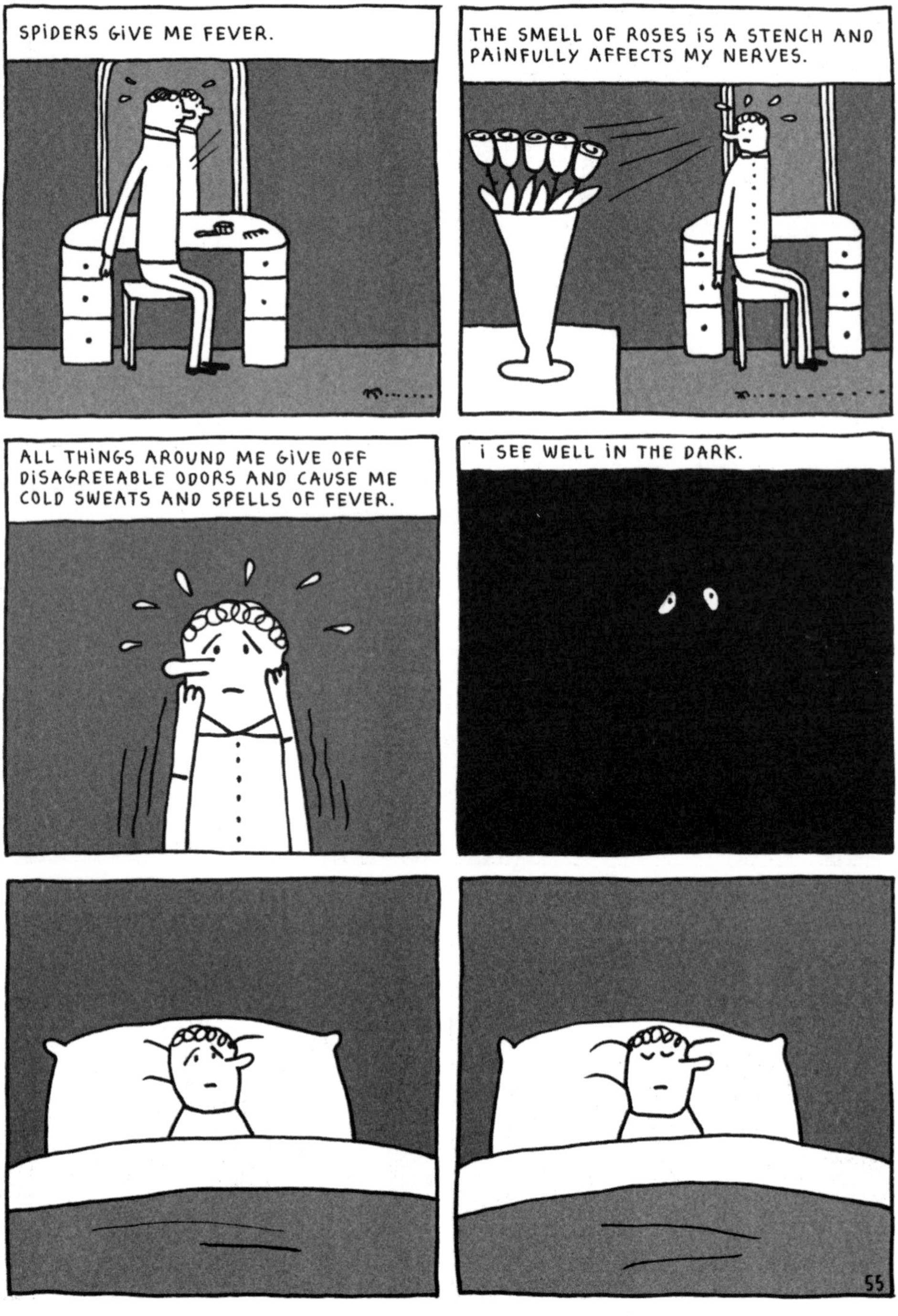
SPIDERS GIVE ME FEVER.
THE SMELL OF ROSES IS A STENCH AND PAINFULLY AFFECTS MY NERVES.
ALL THINGS AROUND ME GIVE OFF DISAGREEABLE ODORS AND CAUSE ME COLD SWEATS AND SPELLS OF FEVER.
I SEE WELL IN THE DARK.

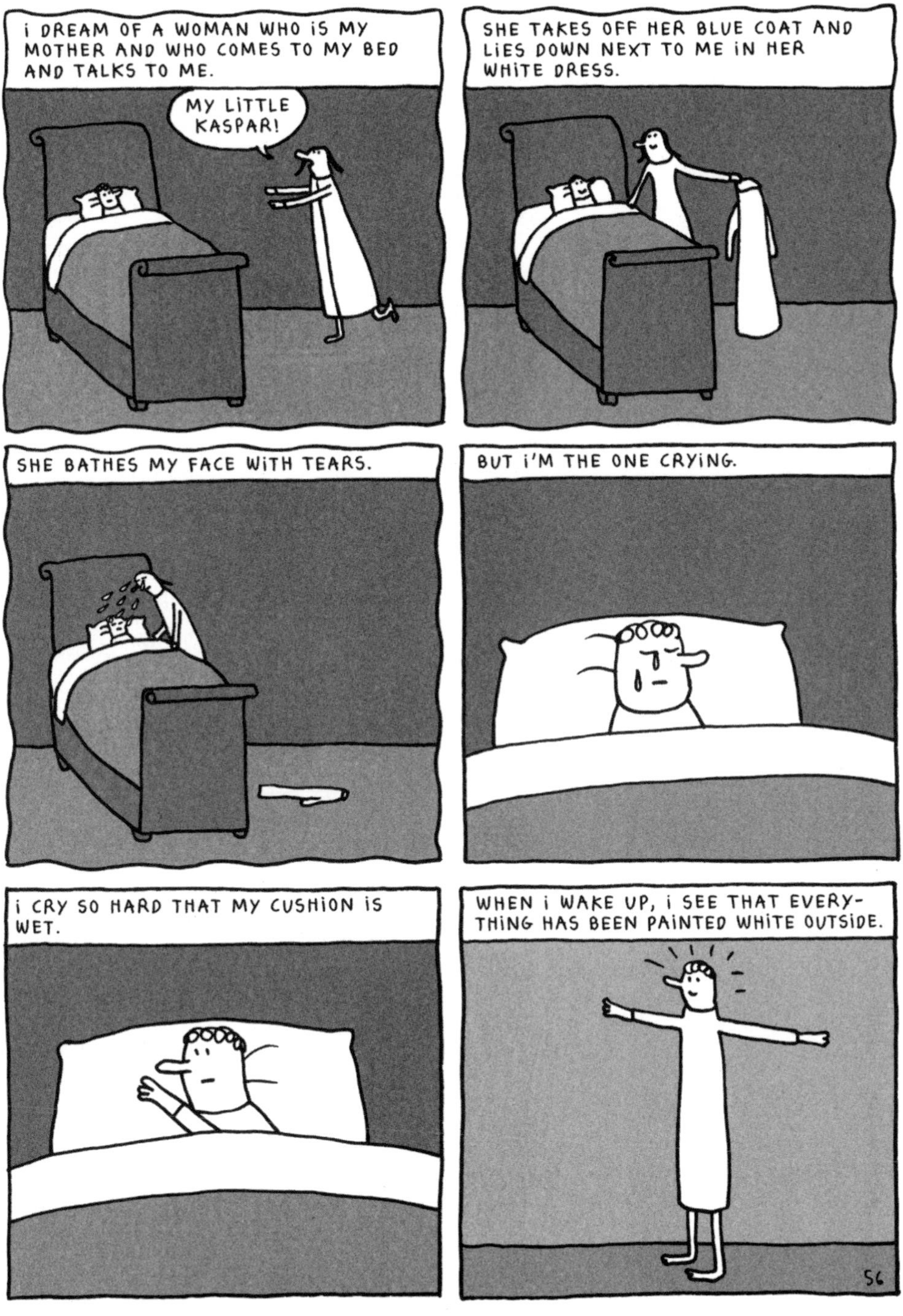
i DREAM OF A WOMAN WHO iS MY MOTHER AND WHO COMES TO MY BED AND TALKS TO ME.
MY LiTTLE KASPAR!
SHE TAKES OFF HER BLUE COAT AND LiES DOWN NEXT TO ME iN HER WHiTE DRESS.
SHE BATHES MY FACE WiTH TEARS.
BUT i'M THE ONE CRYiNG.
i CRY SO HARD THAT MY CUSHiON iS WET.
WHEN i WAKE UP, i SEE THAT EVERY-THiNG HAS BEEN PAiNTED WHiTE OUTSiDE.

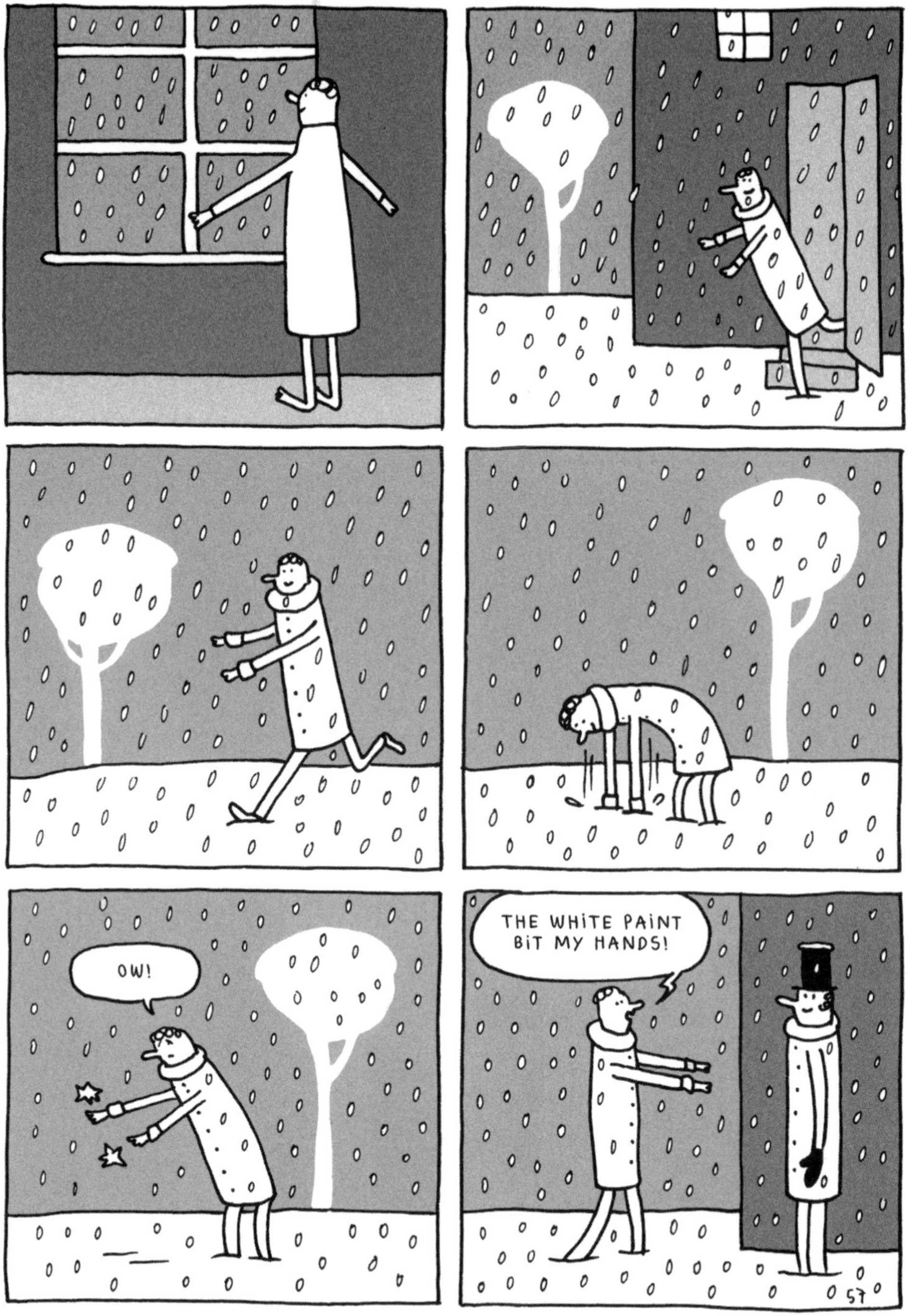
OW!
THE WHITE PAINT BIT MY HANDS!

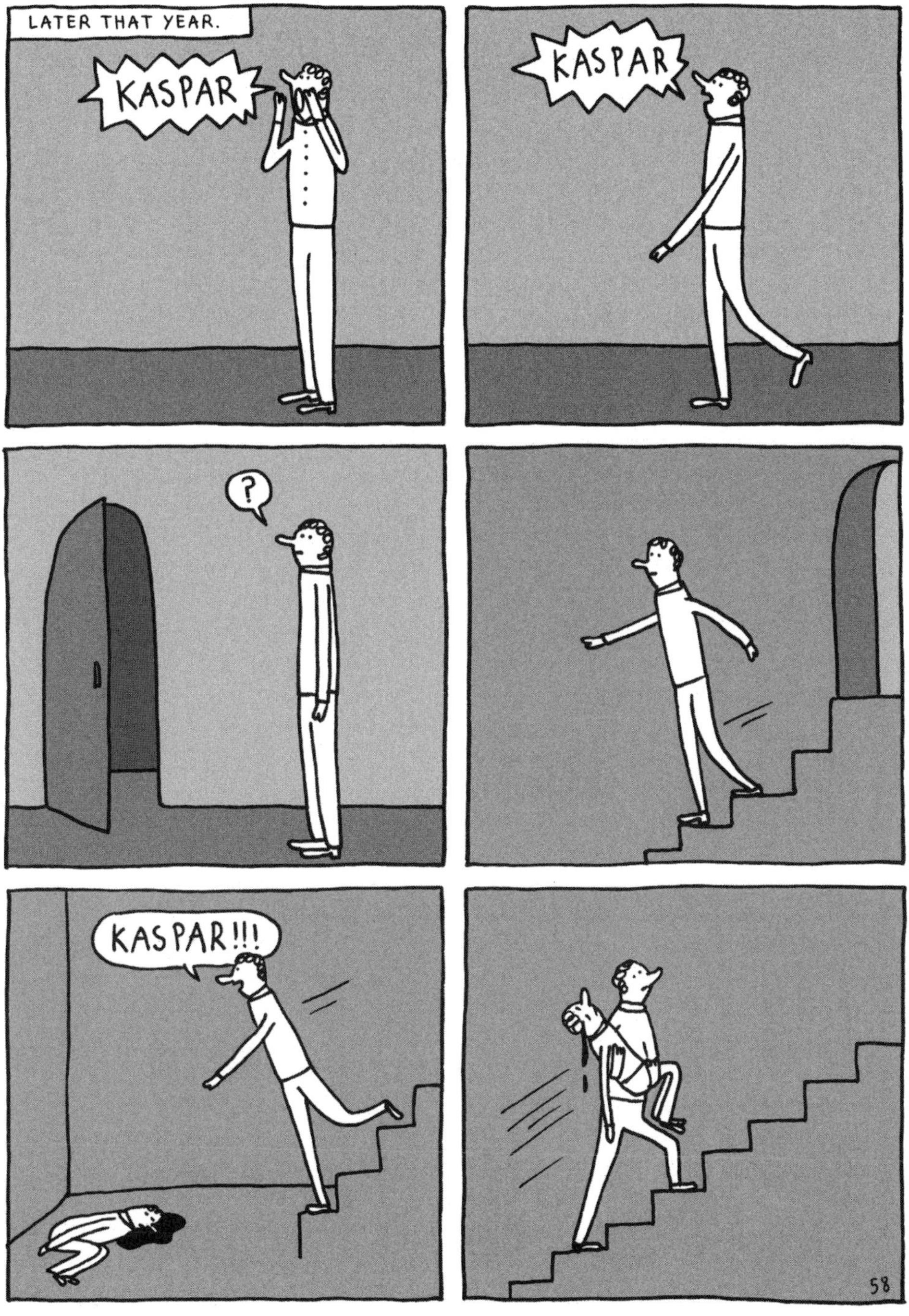
LATER THAT YEAR.
KASPAR
KASPAR
?
KASPAR!!!

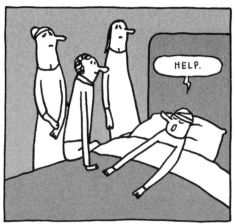

HELP.

SHUSH! IT'S ALRIGHT! YOU'RE SAFE!

TELL US WHAT HAPPENED!

WHILE I WAS IN THE WATER CLOSET, I HEARD THE DOORBELL RING VERY SOFTLY.

I HEARD QUIET FOOTSTEPS.

AND I SAW THAT A MAN HAD SNUCK INTO THE COURTYARD.

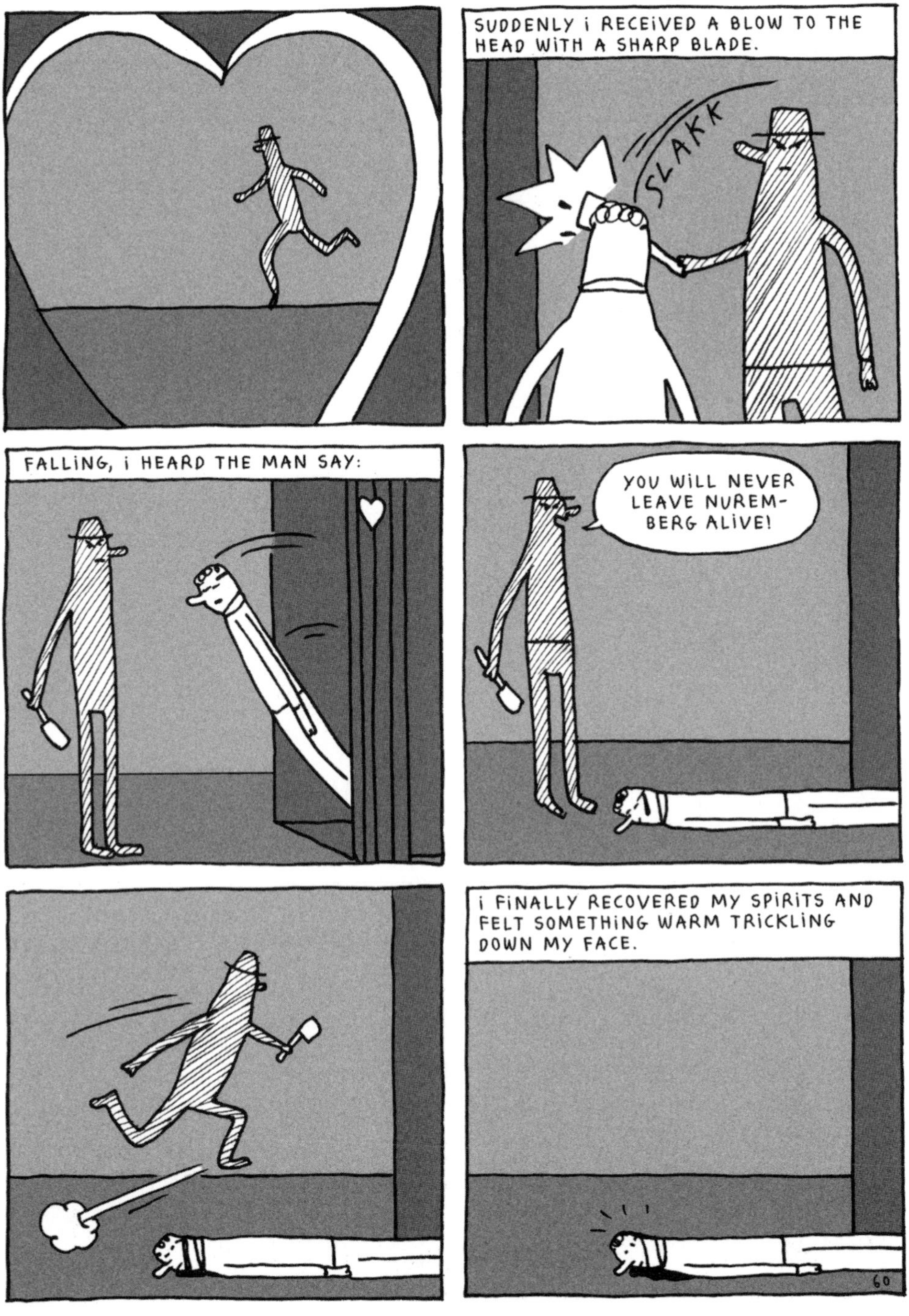
SUDDENLY i RECEiVED A BLOW TO THE HEAD WiTH A SHARP BLADE.
SLAKK
FALLiNG, i HEARD THE MAN SAY:
YOU WiLL NEVER LEAVE NUREM-BERG ALiVE!
i FiNALLY RECOVERED MY SPiRiTS AND FELT SOMETHiNG WARM TRiCKLiNG DOWN MY FACE.

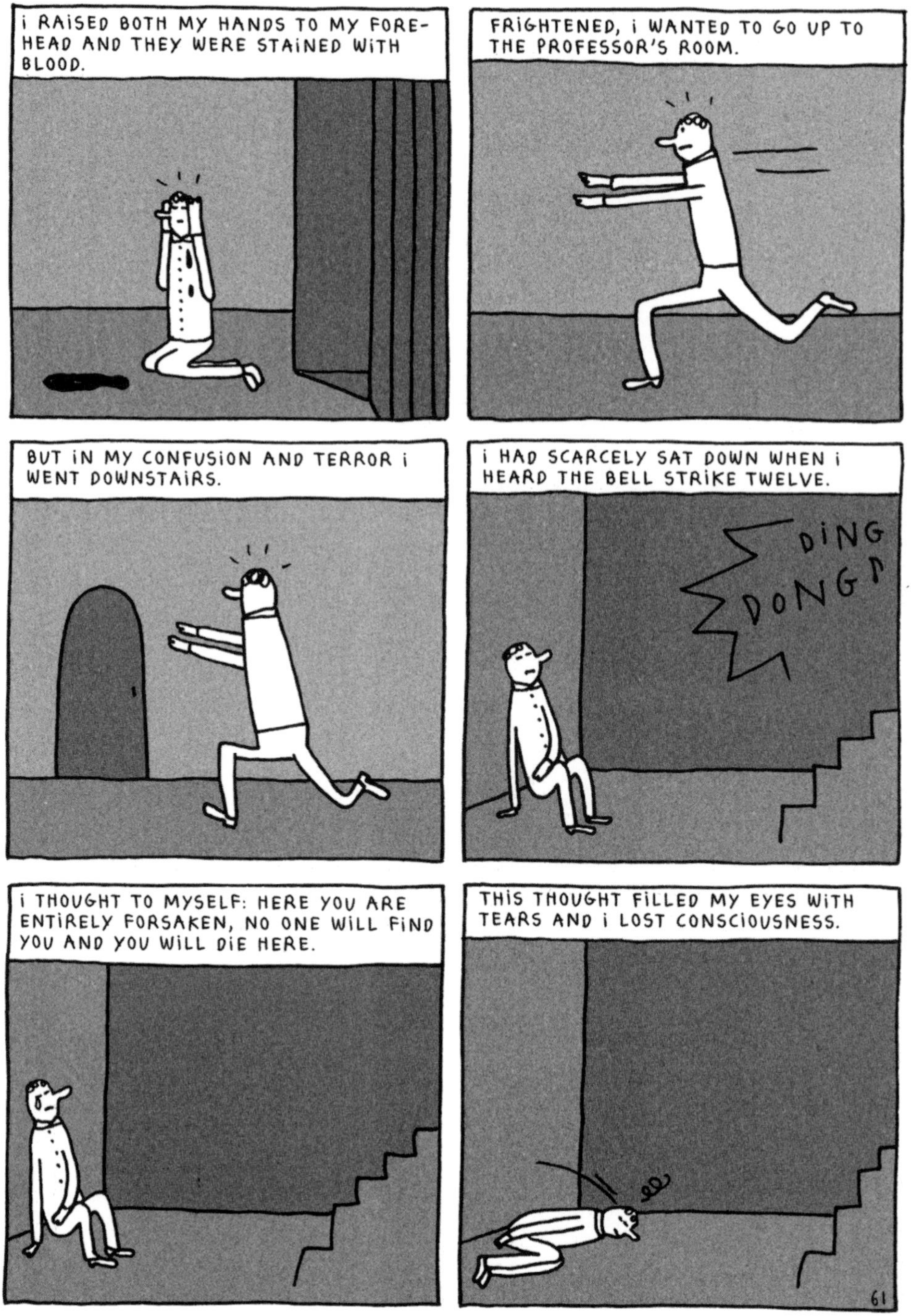
i RAISED BOTH MY HANDS TO MY FORE-HEAD AND THEY WERE STAINED WITH BLOOD.
FRIGHTENED, i WANTED TO GO UP TO THE PROFESSOR'S ROOM.
BUT iN MY CONFUSION AND TERROR i WENT DOWNSTAIRS.
i HAD SCARCELY SAT DOWN WHEN i HEARD THE BELL STRIKE TWELVE.
DING
DONG
i THOUGHT TO MYSELF: HERE YOU ARE ENTIRELY FORSAKEN, NO ONE WILL FIND YOU AND YOU WILL DIE HERE.
THIS THOUGHT FILLED MY EYES WITH TEARS AND i LOST CONSCIOUSNESS.

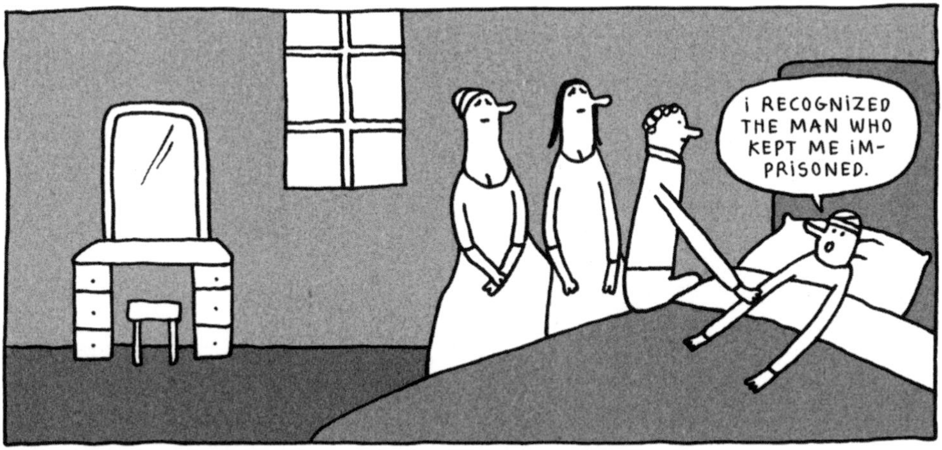
I RECOGNIZED THE MAN WHO KEPT ME IM-PRISONED.

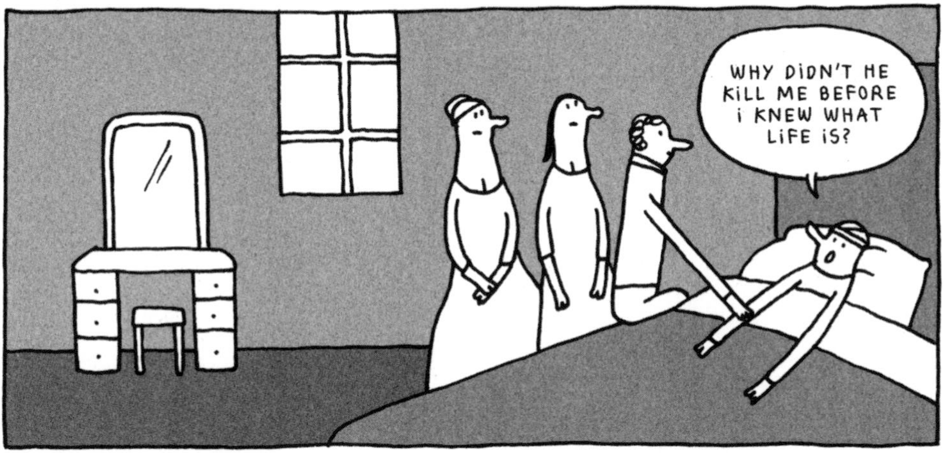
WHY DIDN'T HE KILL ME BEFORE I KNEW WHAT LIFE IS?

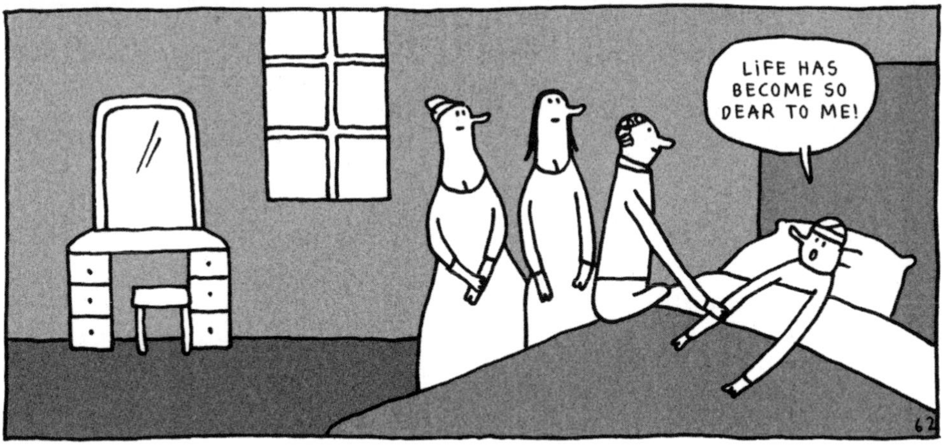
LIFE HAS BECOME SO DEAR TO ME!

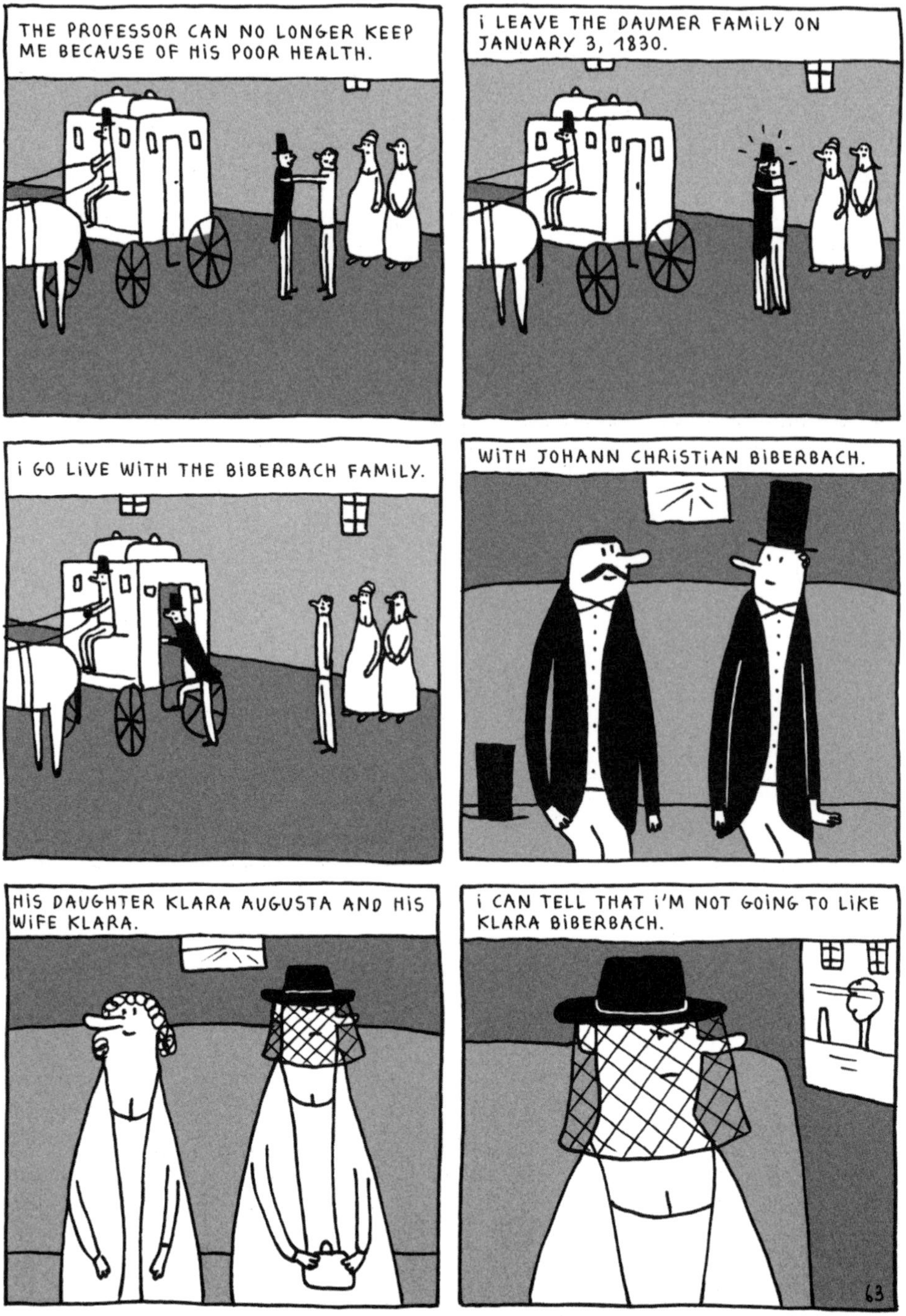
THE PROFESSOR CAN NO LONGER KEEP ME BECAUSE OF HIS POOR HEALTH.
I LEAVE THE DAUMER FAMILY ON JANUARY 3, 1830.
I GO LIVE WITH THE BIBERBACH FAMILY.
WITH JOHANN CHRISTIAN BIBERBACH.
HIS DAUGHTER KLARA AUGUSTA AND HIS WIFE KLARA.
I CAN TELL THAT I'M NOT GOING TO LIKE KLARA BIBERBACH.

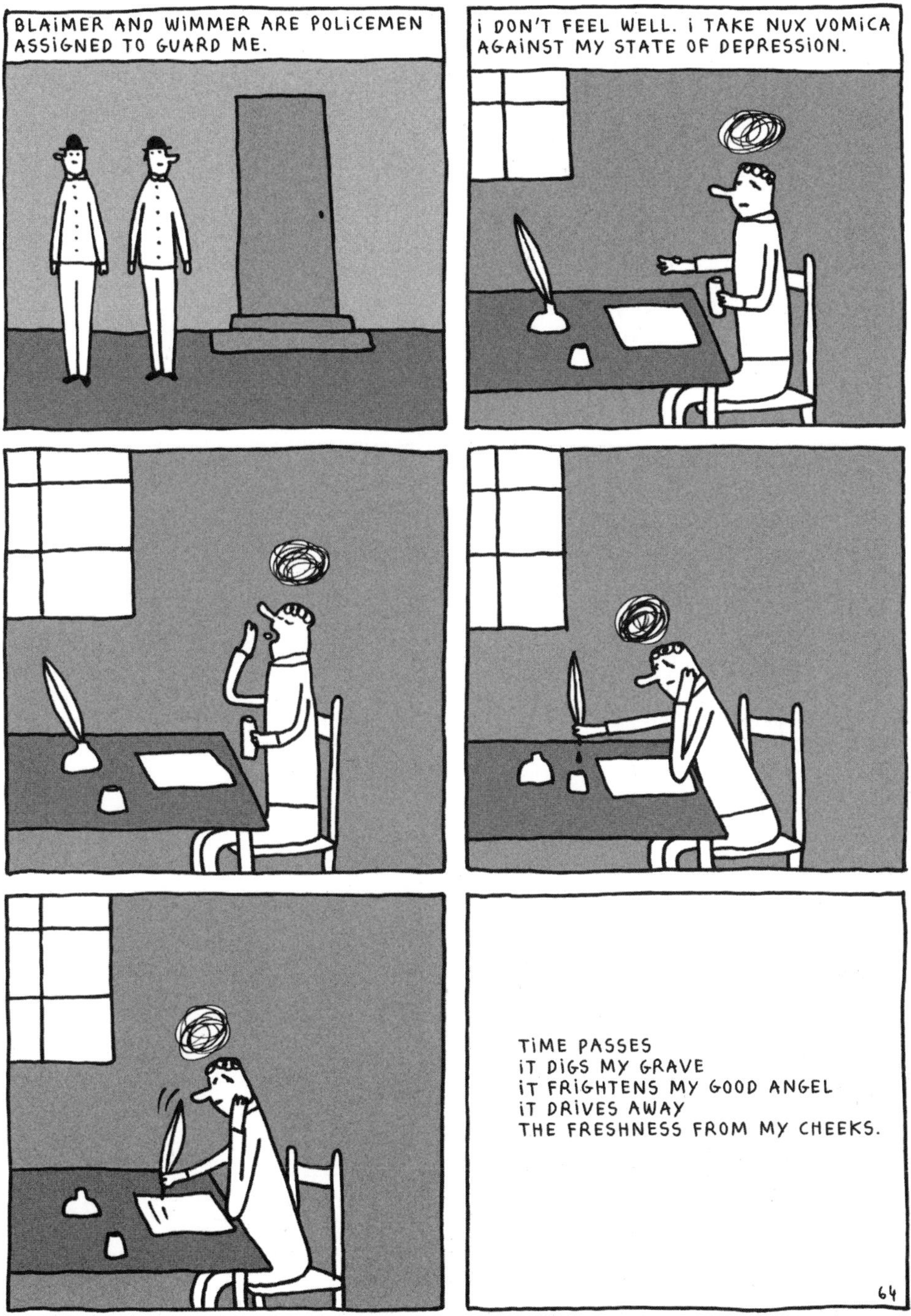
BLAIMER AND WIMMER ARE POLICEMEN ASSIGNED TO GUARD ME.
I DON'T FEEL WELL. I TAKE NUX VOMICA AGAINST MY STATE OF DEPRESSION.
TIME PASSES
IT DIGS MY GRAVE
IT FRIGHTENS MY GOOD ANGEL
IT DRIVES AWAY
THE FRESHNESS FROM MY CHEEKS.

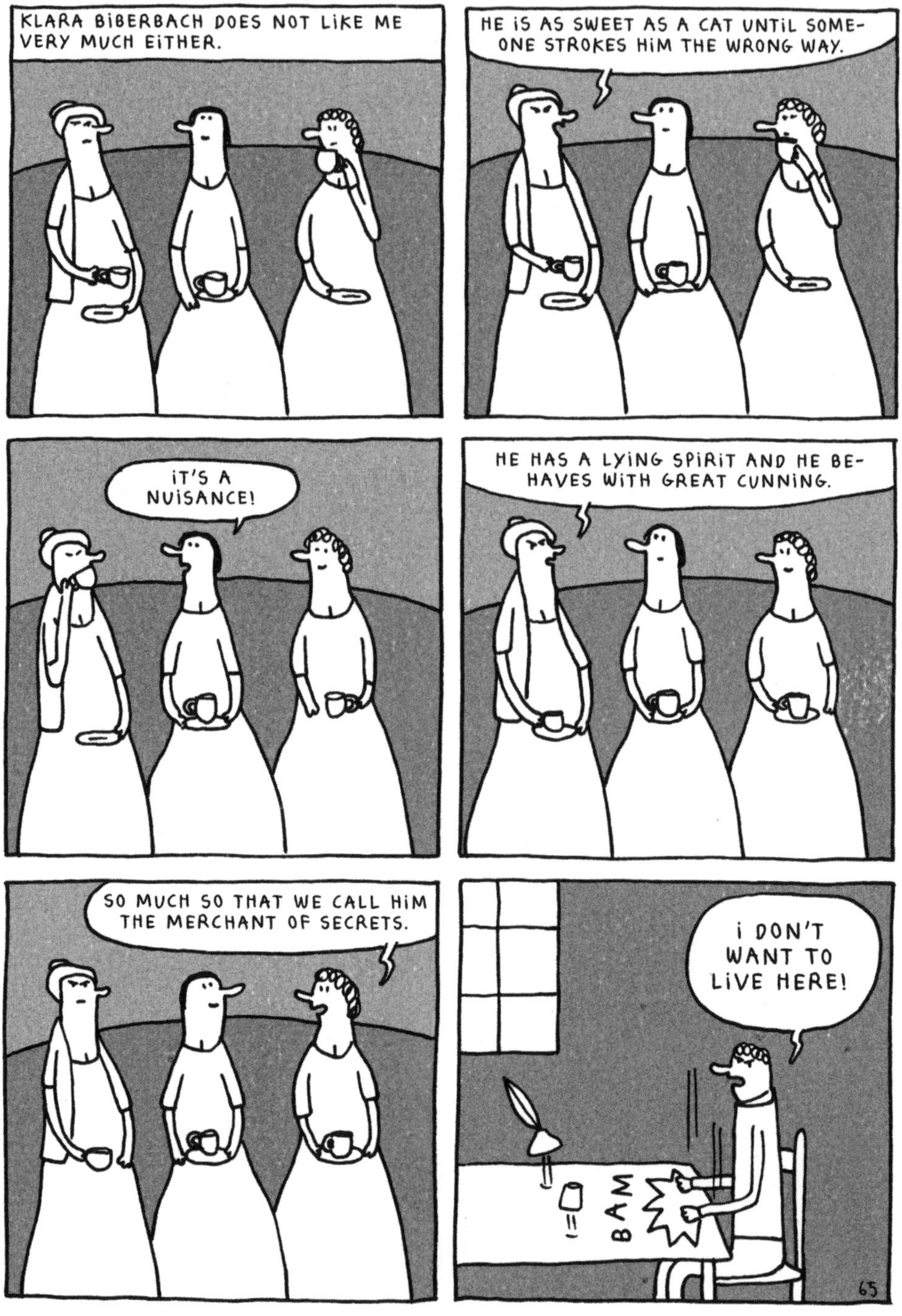
KLARA BIBERBACH DOES NOT LIKE ME VERY MUCH EITHER.
HE IS AS SWEET AS A CAT UNTIL SOME-ONE STROKES HIM THE WRONG WAY.
IT'S A NUISANCE!
HE HAS A LYING SPIRIT AND HE BE-HAVES WITH GREAT CUNNING.
SO MUCH SO THAT WE CALL HIM THE MERCHANT OF SECRETS.
I DON'T WANT TO LIVE HERE!
BAM
!!

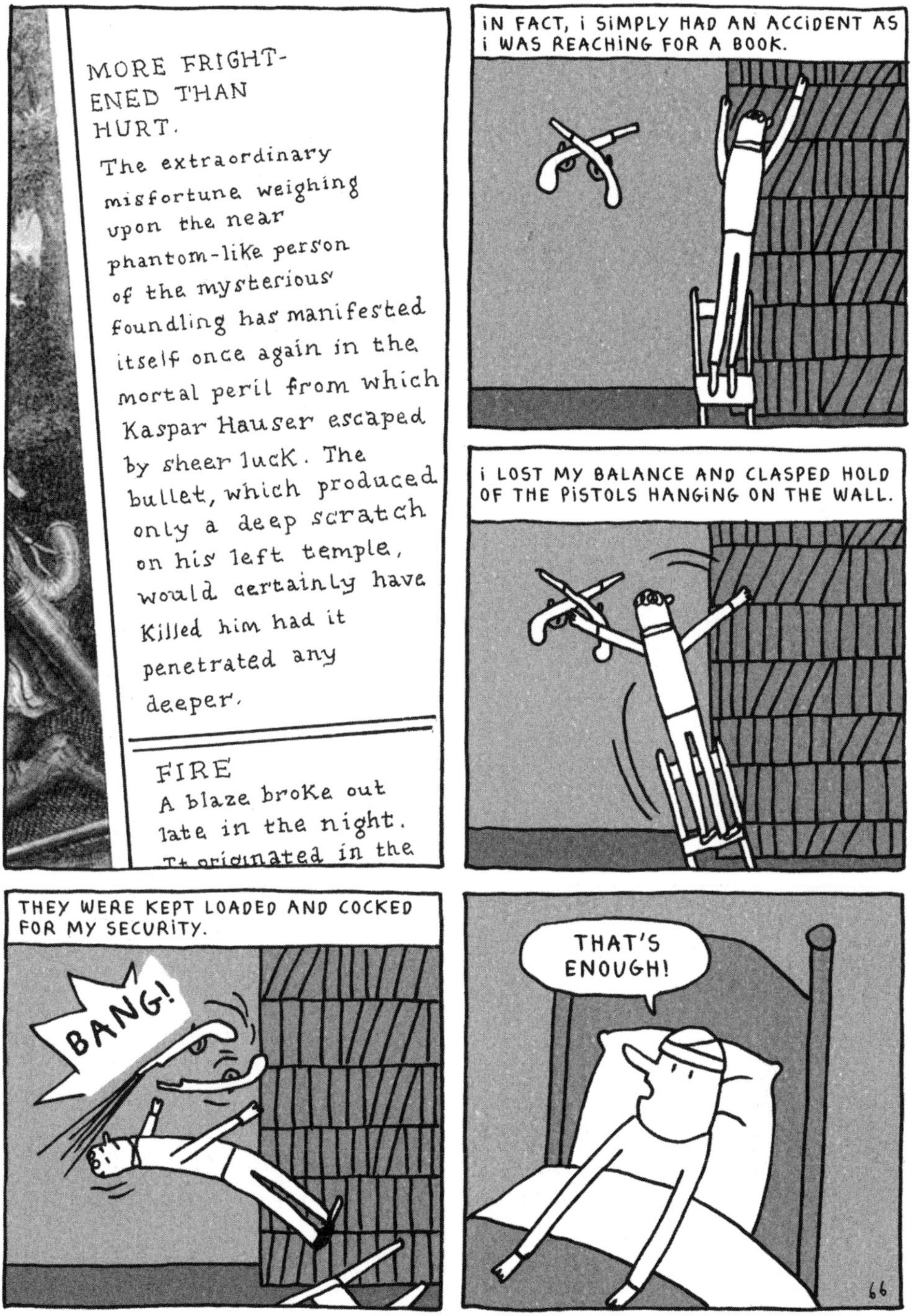
MORE FRIGHT-
ENED THAN
HURT.
The extraordinary misfortune weighing upon the near phantom-like person of the mysterious foundling has manifested itself once again in the mortal peril from which Kaspar Hauser escaped by sheer luck. The bullet, which produced only a deep scratch on his left temple, would certainly have killed him had it penetrated any deeper.
FIRE
A blaze broke out late in the night.
IN FACT, I SIMPLY HAD AN ACCIDENT AS I WAS REACHING FOR A BOOK.
I LOST MY BALANCE AND CLASPED HOLD OF THE PISTOLS HANGING ON THE WALL.
THEY WERE KEPT LOADED AND COCKED FOR MY SECURITY.
BANG!
THAT'S ENOUGH!

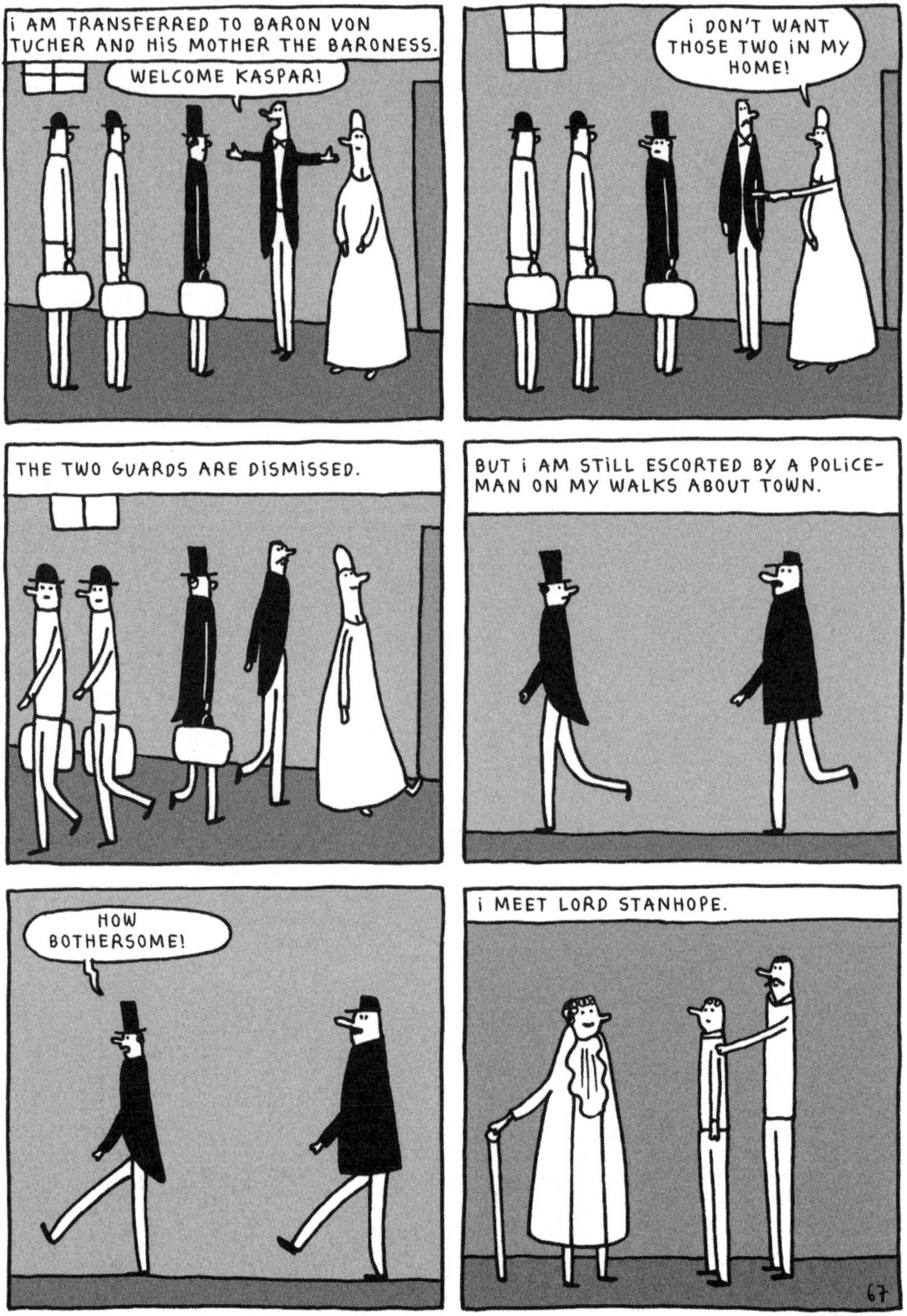
I AM TRANSFERRED TO BARON VON TUCHER AND HIS MOTHER THE BARONESS.
WELCOME KASPAR!
I DON'T WANT THOSE TWO IN MY HOME!
THE TWO GUARDS ARE DISMISSED.
BUT I AM STILL ESCORTED BY A POLICE-MAN ON MY WALKS ABOUT TOWN.
HOW BOTHERSOME!
I MEET LORD STANHOPE.

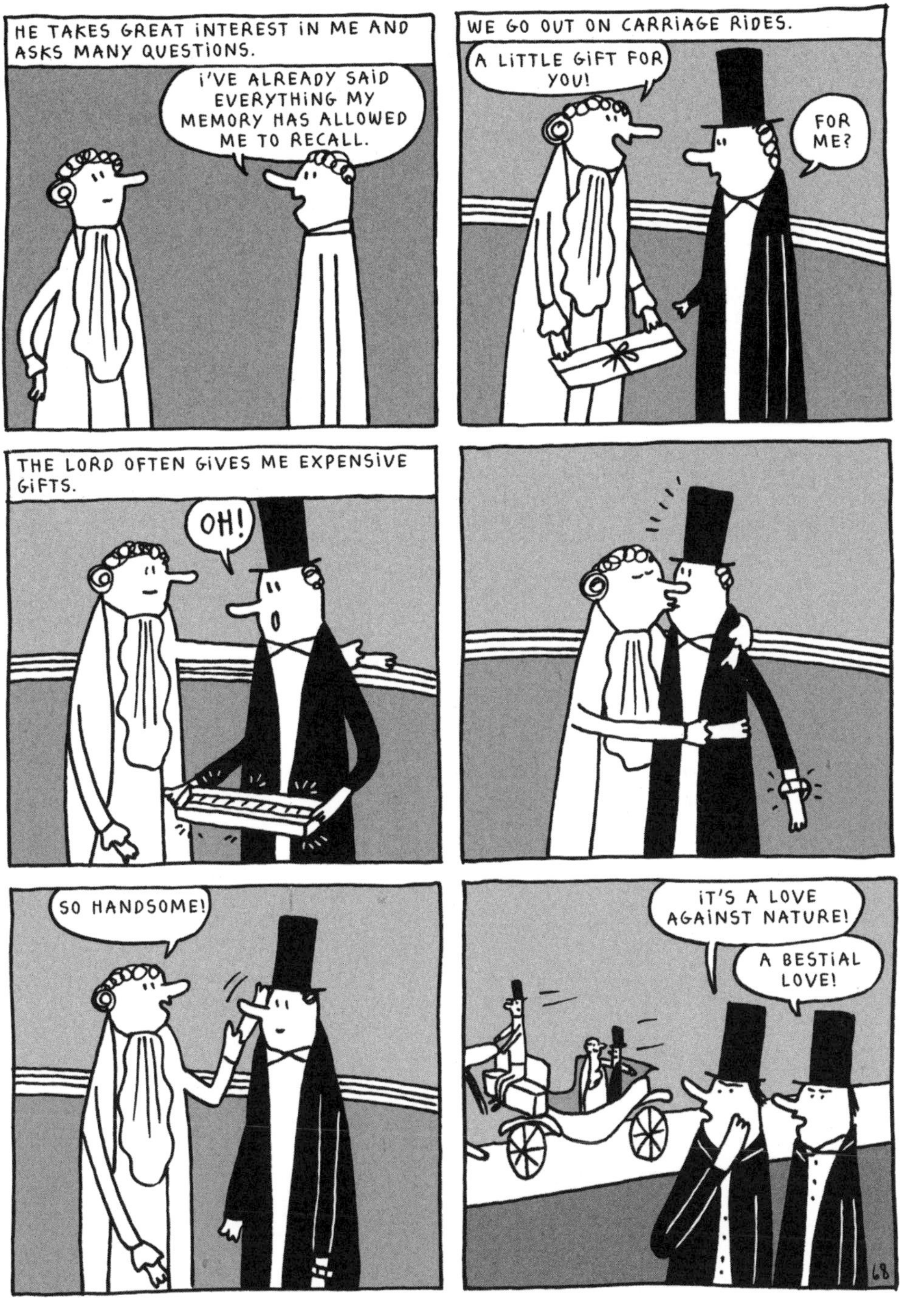
HE TAKES GREAT INTEREST IN ME AND ASKS MANY QUESTIONS.
I'VE ALREADY SAID EVERYTHING MY MEMORY HAS ALLOWED ME TO RECALL.
WE GO OUT ON CARRIAGE RIDES.
A LITTLE GIFT FOR YOU!
FOR ME?
THE LORD OFTEN GIVES ME EXPENSIVE GIFTS.
OH!
SO HANDSOME!
IT'S A LOVE AGAINST NATURE!
A BESTIAL LOVE!

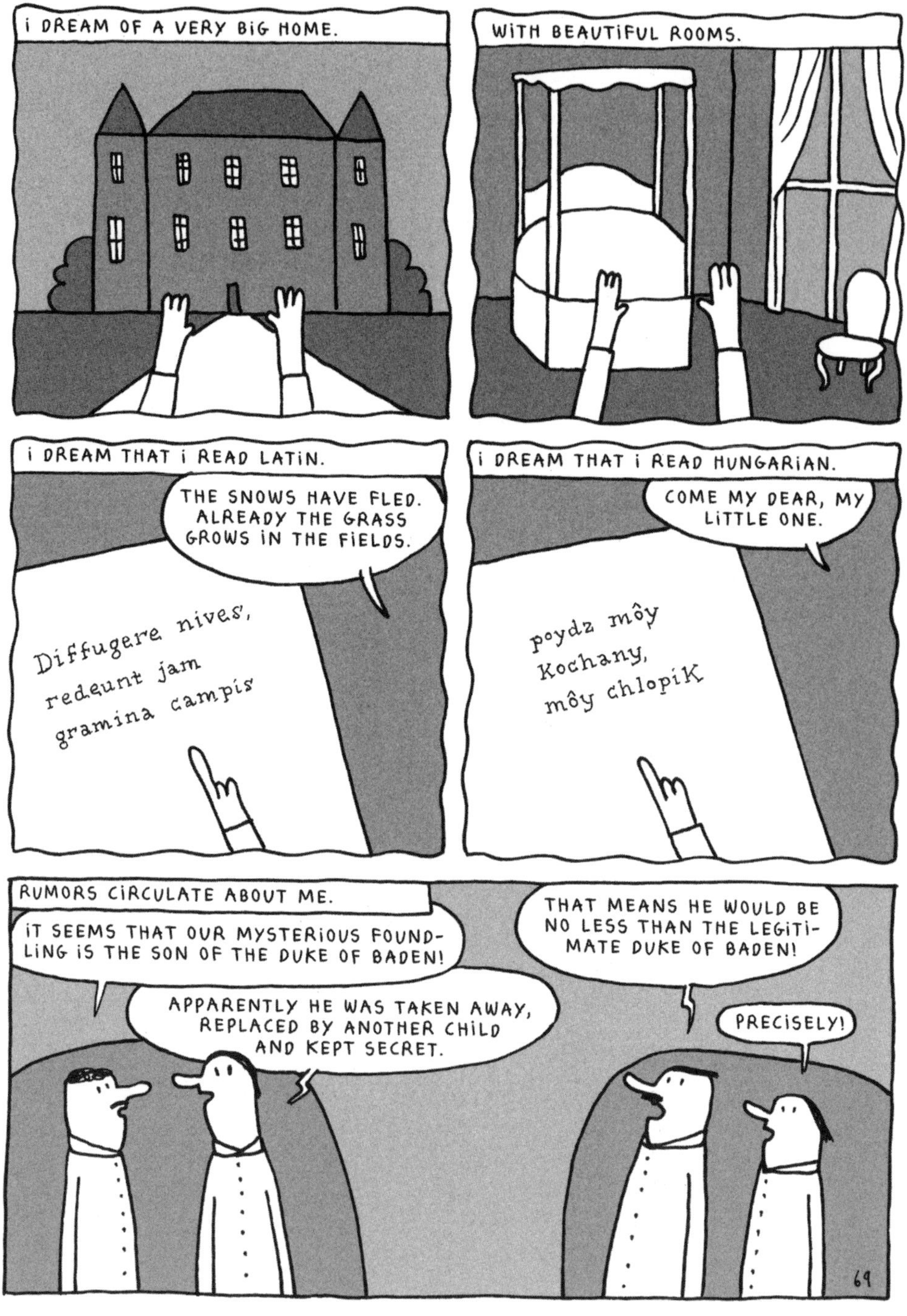
i DREAM OF A VERY BiG HOME.
WiTH BEAUTiFUL ROOMS.
i DREAM THAT i READ LATiN.
THE SNOWS HAVE FLED. ALREADY THE GRASS GROWS iN THE FiELDS.
Diffugere nives, redeunt jam gramina campis
i DREAM THAT i READ HUNGARiAN.
COME MY DEAR, MY LiTTLE ONE.
poydz môy Kochany, môy chlopiK
RUMORS CiRCULATE ABOUT ME.
iT SEEMS THAT OUR MYSTERiOUS FOUND-LiNG iS THE SON OF THE DUKE OF BADEN!
APPARENTLY HE WAS TAKEN AWAY, REPLACED BY ANOTHER CHiLD AND KEPT SECRET.
THAT MEANS HE WOULD BE NO LESS THAN THE LEGiTi-MATE DUKE OF BADEN!
PRECiSELY!

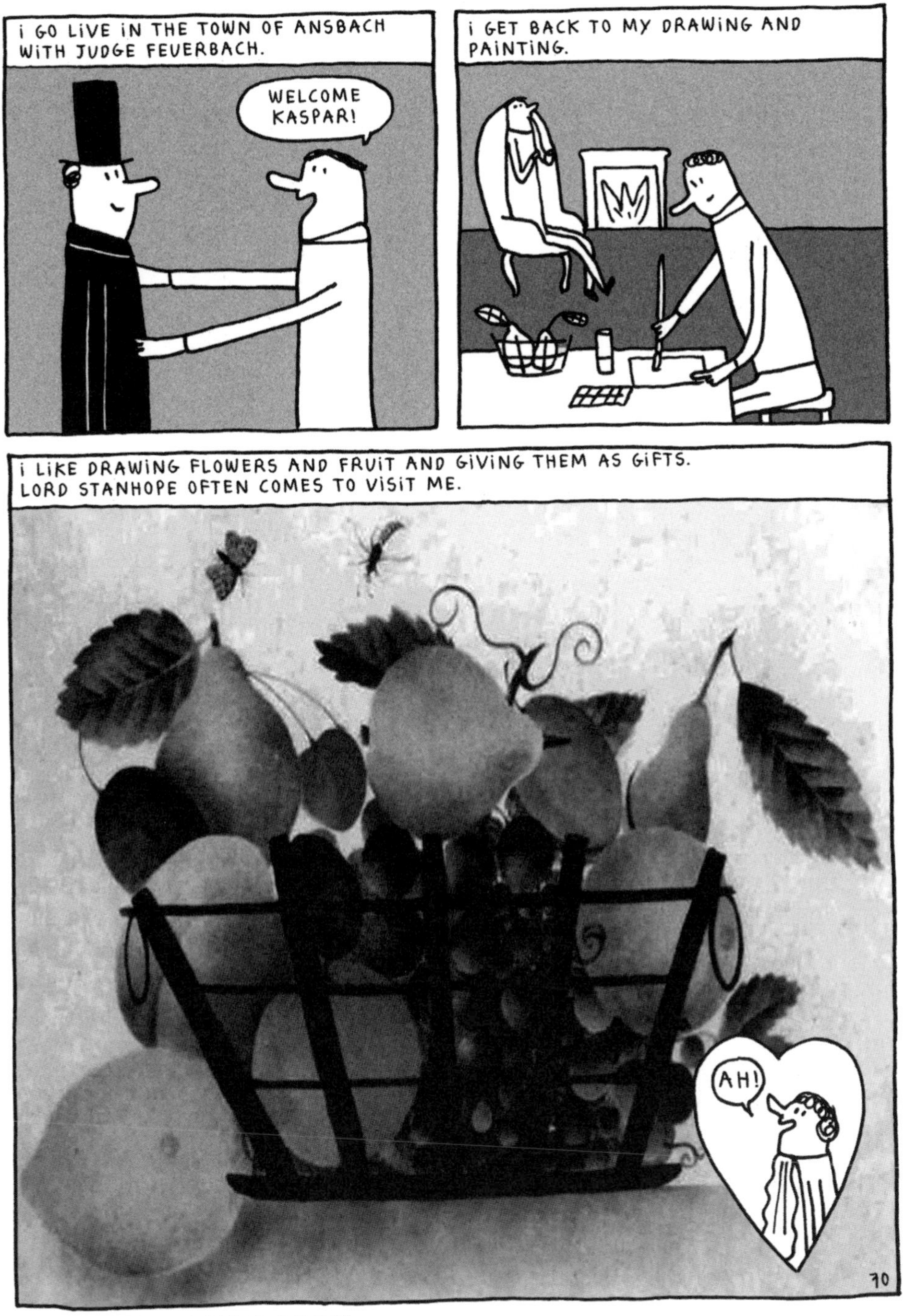
i GO LiVE iN THE TOWN OF ANSBACH WiTH JUDGE FEUERBACH.
WELCOME KASPAR!
i GET BACK TO MY DRAWiNG AND PAiNTiNG.
i LiKE DRAWiNG FLOWERS AND FRUiT AND GiViNG THEM AS GiFTS. LORD STANHOPE OFTEN COMES TO ViSiT ME.
AH!

WATERCOLOR BY KASPAR HAUSER

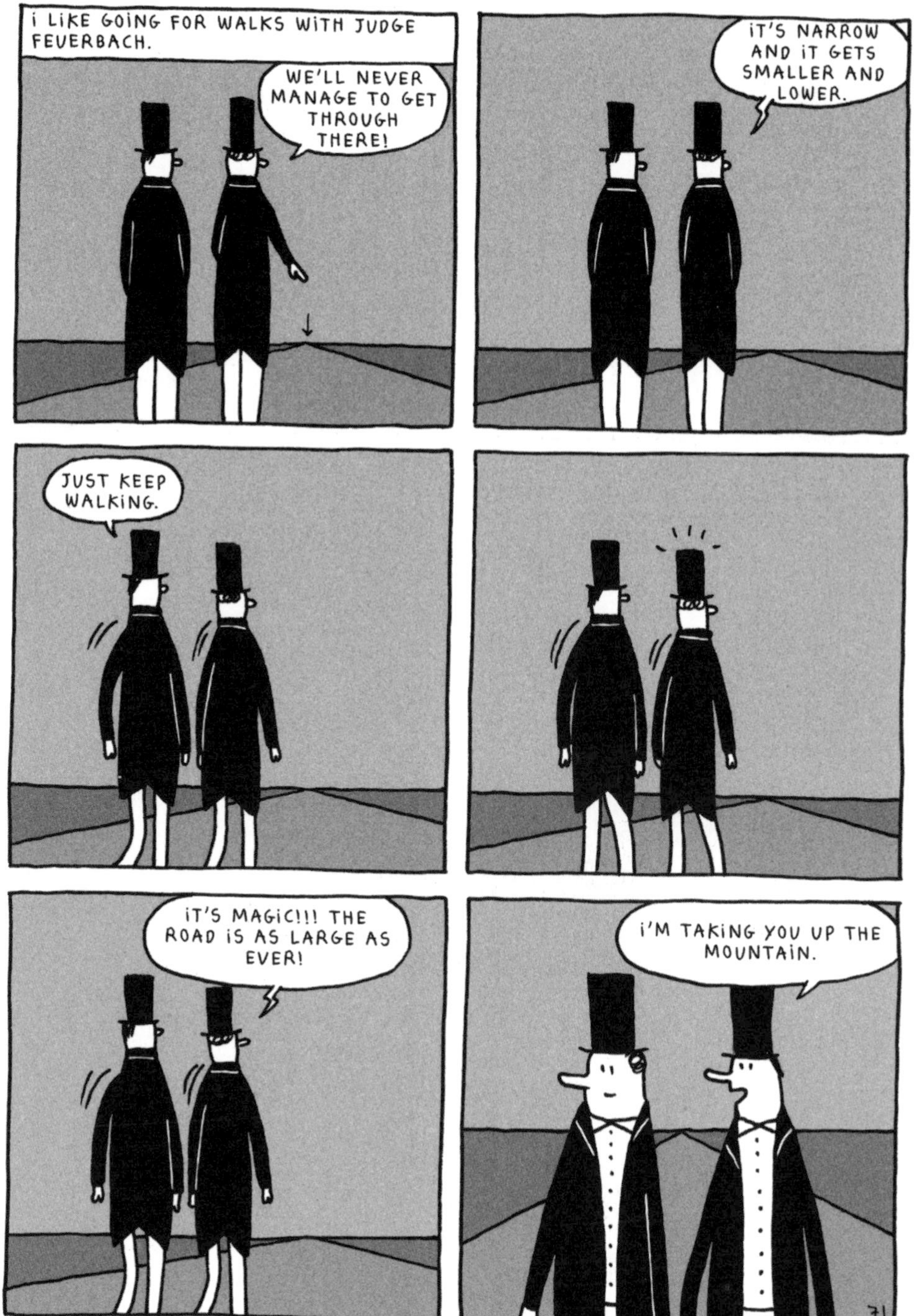
I LIKE GOING FOR WALKS WITH JUDGE FEUERBACH.
WE'LL NEVER MANAGE TO GET THROUGH THERE!
IT'S NARROW AND IT GETS SMALLER AND LOWER.
JUST KEEP WALKING.
IT'S MAGIC!!! THE ROAD IS AS LARGE AS EVER!
I'M TAKING YOU UP THE MOUNTAIN.

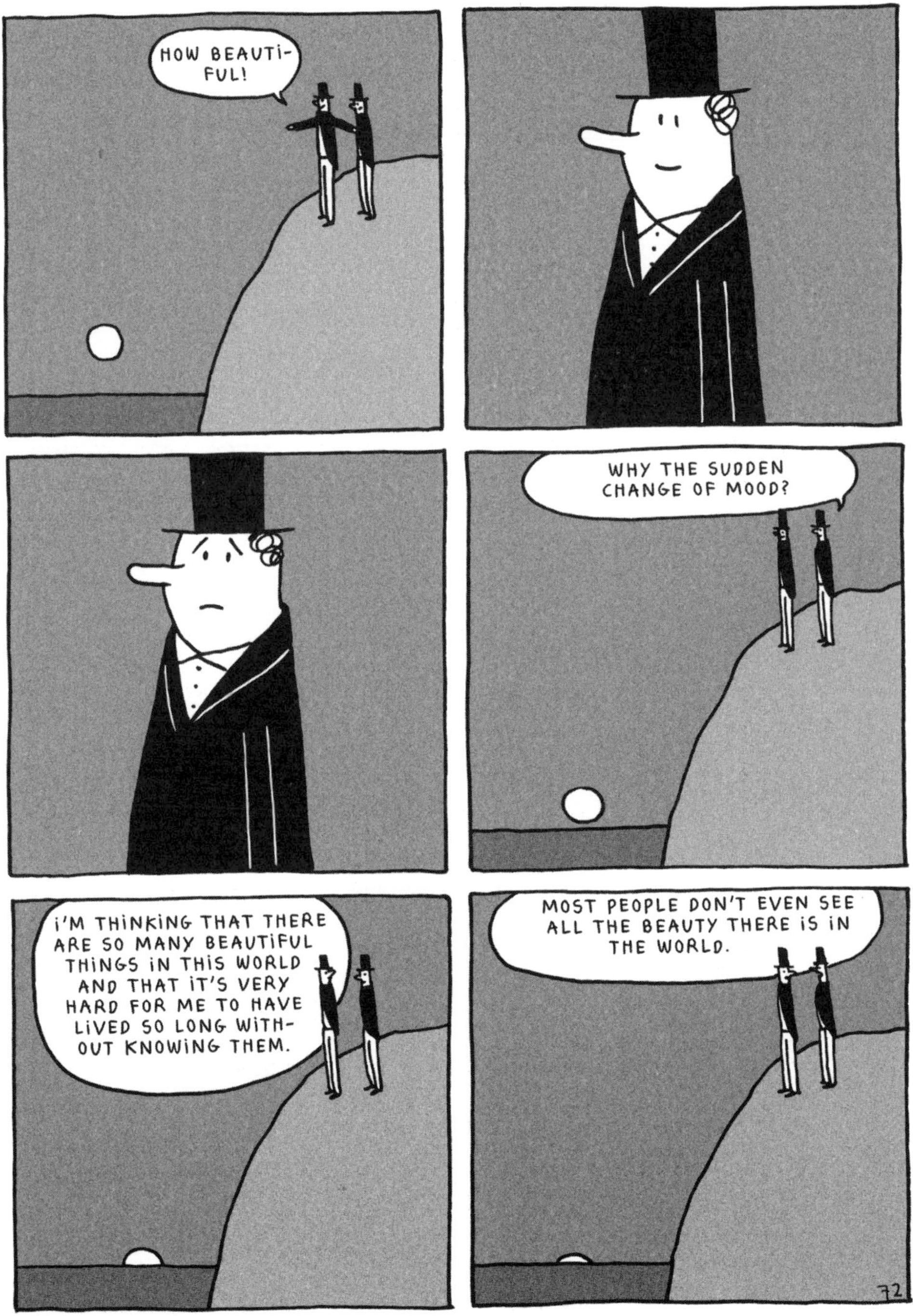
HOW BEAUTI-
FUL!
WHY THE SUDDEN
CHANGE OF MOOD?
I'M THINKING THAT THERE ARE SO MANY BEAUTIFUL THINGS IN THIS WORLD AND THAT IT'S VERY HARD FOR ME TO HAVE LIVED SO LONG WITH-OUT KNOWING THEM.
MOST PEOPLE DON'T EVEN SEE ALL THE BEAUTY THERE IS IN THE WORLD.
72

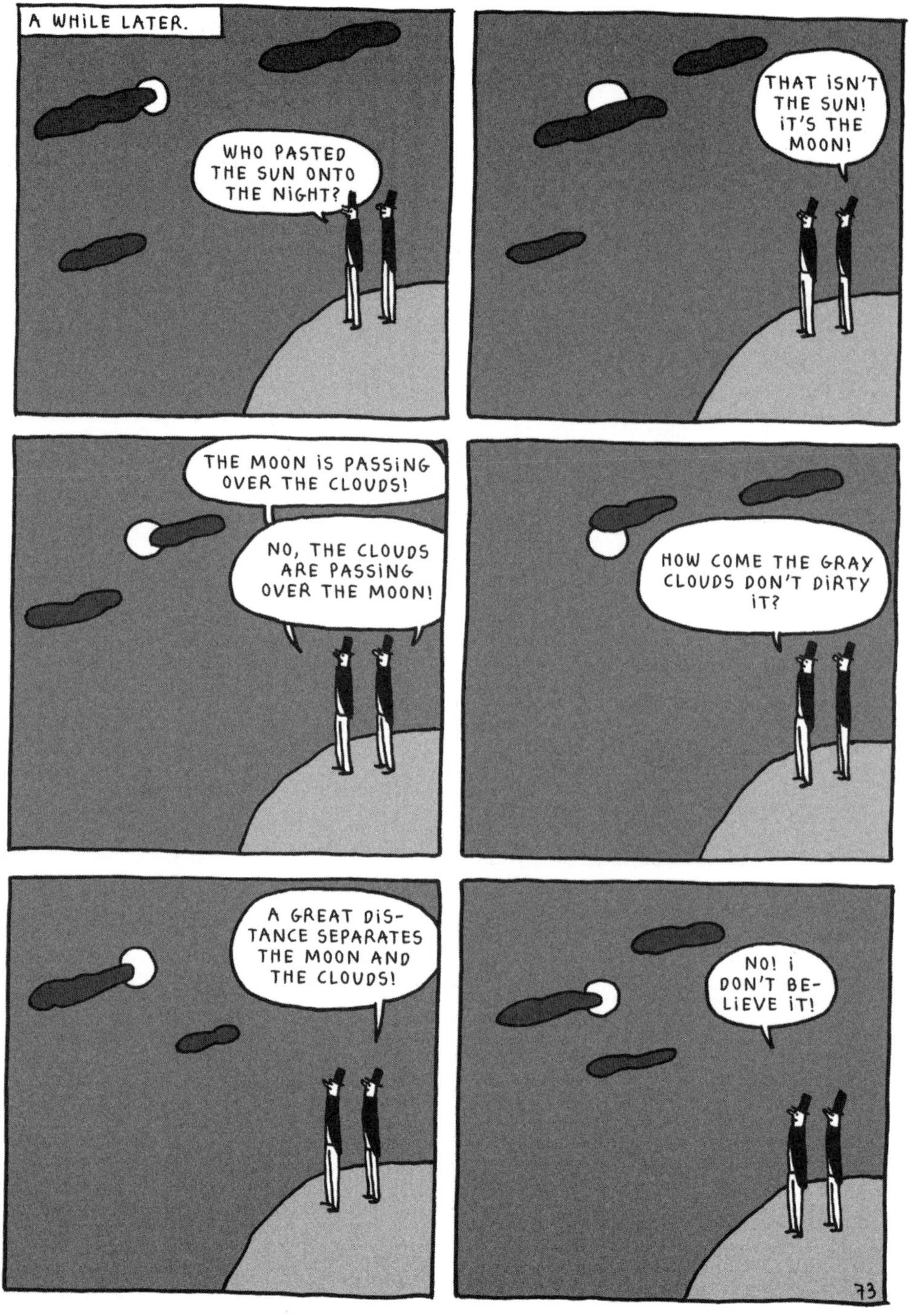
A WHILE LATER.
WHO PASTED THE SUN ONTO THE NIGHT?
THAT ISN'T THE SUN! IT'S THE MOON!
THE MOON IS PASSING OVER THE CLOUDS!
NO, THE CLOUDS ARE PASSING OVER THE MOON!
HOW COME THE GRAY CLOUDS DON'T DIRTY IT?
A GREAT DIS-TANCE SEPARATES THE MOON AND THE CLOUDS!
NO! I DON'T BE-LIEVE IT!
73

I GO TO LIVE WITH PROFESSOR JOHANN GEORG MEYER AND HIS WIFE HENRIETTE.

WELCOME KASPAR.

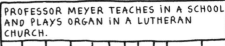

PROFESSOR MEYER TEACHES IN A SCHOOL AND PLAYS ORGAN IN A LUTHERAN CHURCH.

I HAVE A SMALL ROOM.

YOU NEED TO STUDY!

MY MIND SUFFERS A SECOND IMPRISONMENT WITH THE LEARNING OF LATIN.

WHAT GOOD IS ALL THIS LATIN FOR ME?

ONE MUST LEARN LATIN TO KNOW GERMAN!

DID THE ROMANS LEARN GERMAN TO READ AND WRITE LATIN?

74

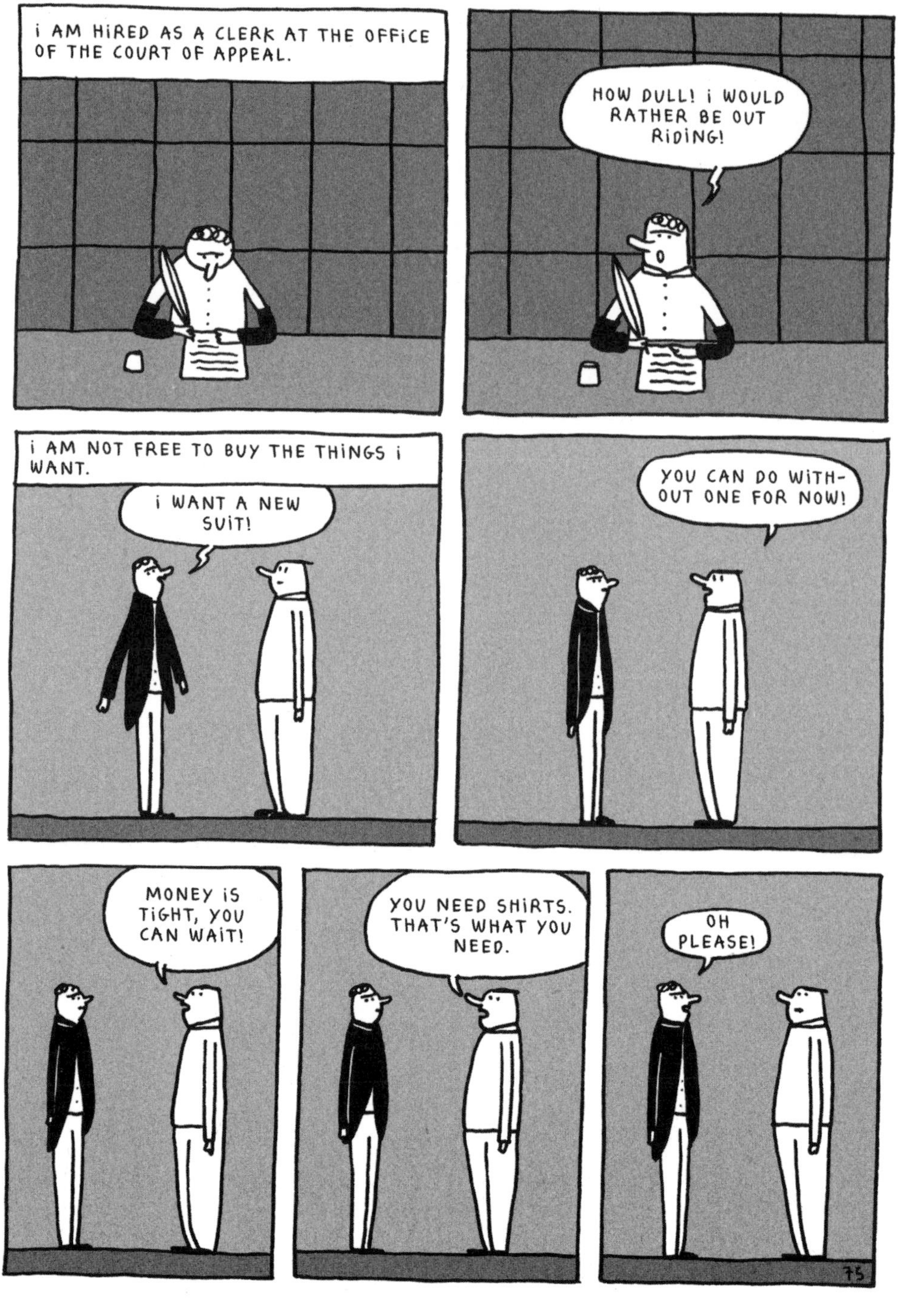

i AM HiRED AS A CLERK AT THE OFFiCE OF THE COURT OF APPEAL.
HOW DULL! i WOULD RATHER BE OUT RiDiNG!
i AM NOT FREE TO BUY THE THiNGS i WANT.
i WANT A NEW SUiT!
YOU CAN DO WiTH-OUT ONE FOR NOW!
MONEY iS TiGHT, YOU CAN WAiT!
YOU NEED SHiRTS. THAT'S WHAT YOU NEED.
OH PLEASE!

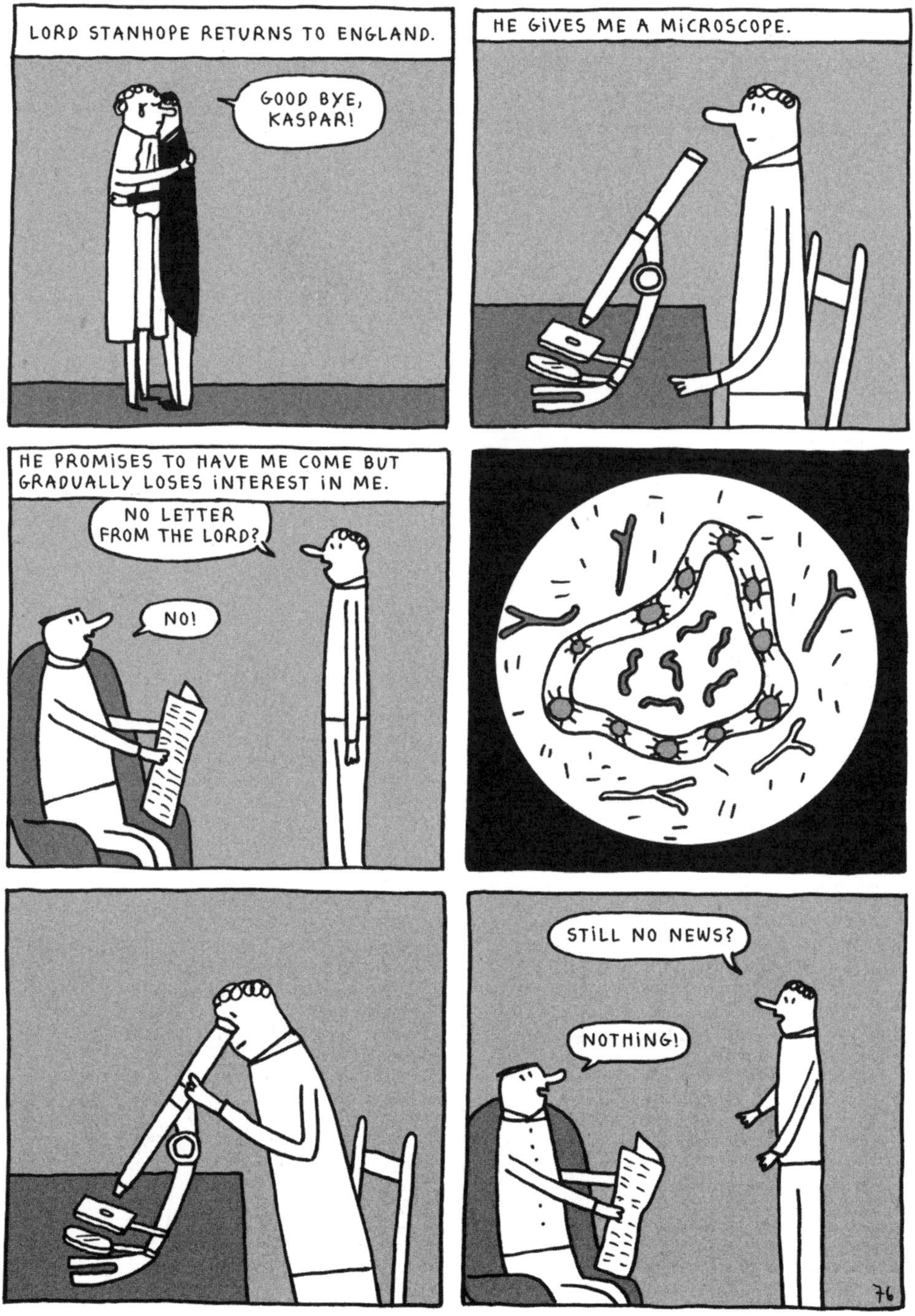
LORD STANHOPE RETURNS TO ENGLAND.
GOOD BYE, KASPAR!
HE GIVES ME A MICROSCOPE.
HE PROMISES TO HAVE ME COME BUT GRADUALLY LOSES INTEREST IN ME.
NO LETTER FROM THE LORD?
NO!
STILL NO NEWS?
NOTHING!

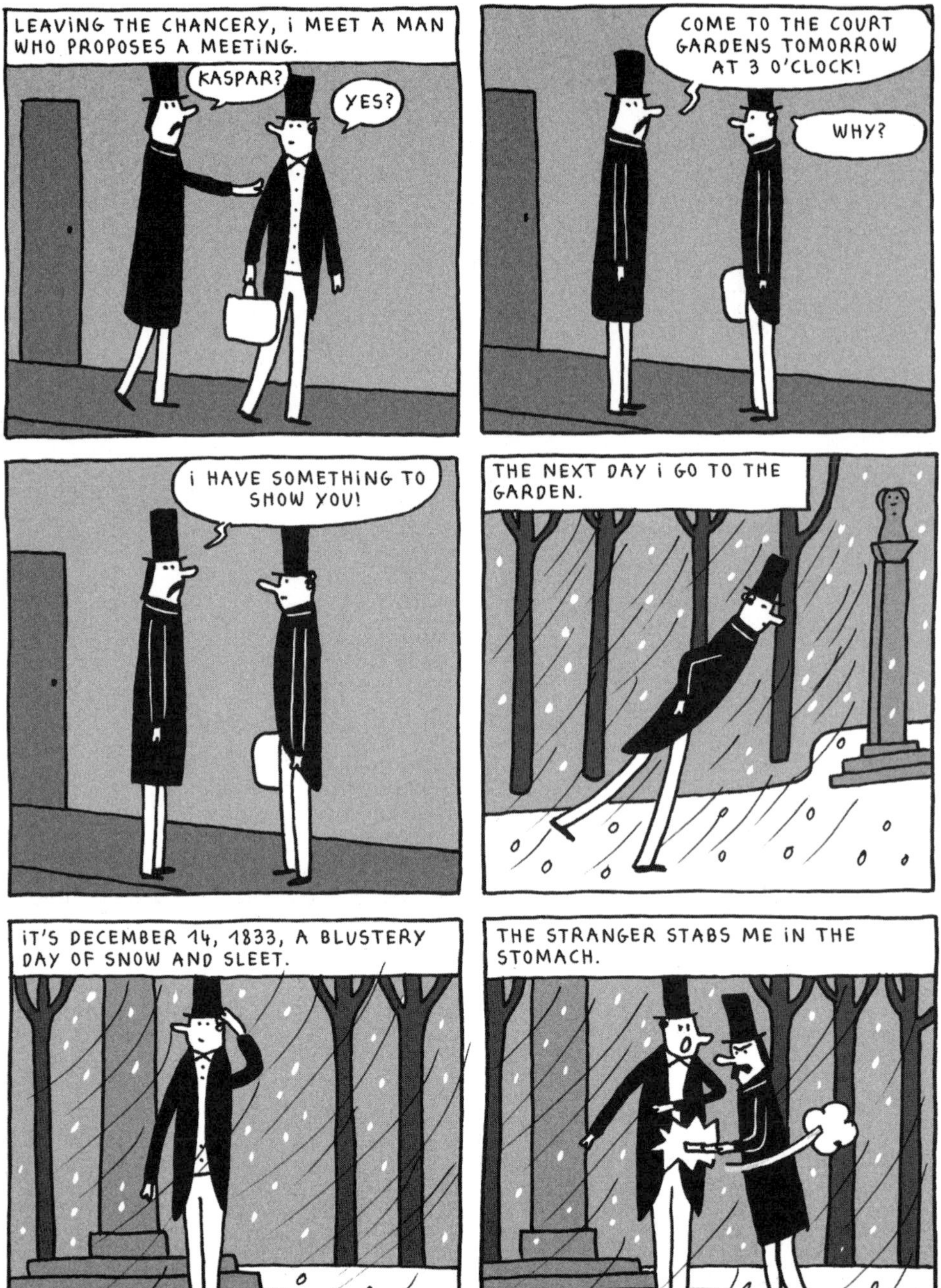
LEAVING THE CHANCERY, I MEET A MAN WHO PROPOSES A MEETING.
KASPAR?
YES?
COME TO THE COURT GARDENS TOMORROW AT 3 O'CLOCK!
WHY?
I HAVE SOMETHING TO SHOW YOU!
THE NEXT DAY I GO TO THE GARDEN.
IT'S DECEMBER 14, 1833, A BLUSTERY DAY OF SNOW AND SLEET.
THE STRANGER STABS ME IN THE STOMACH.

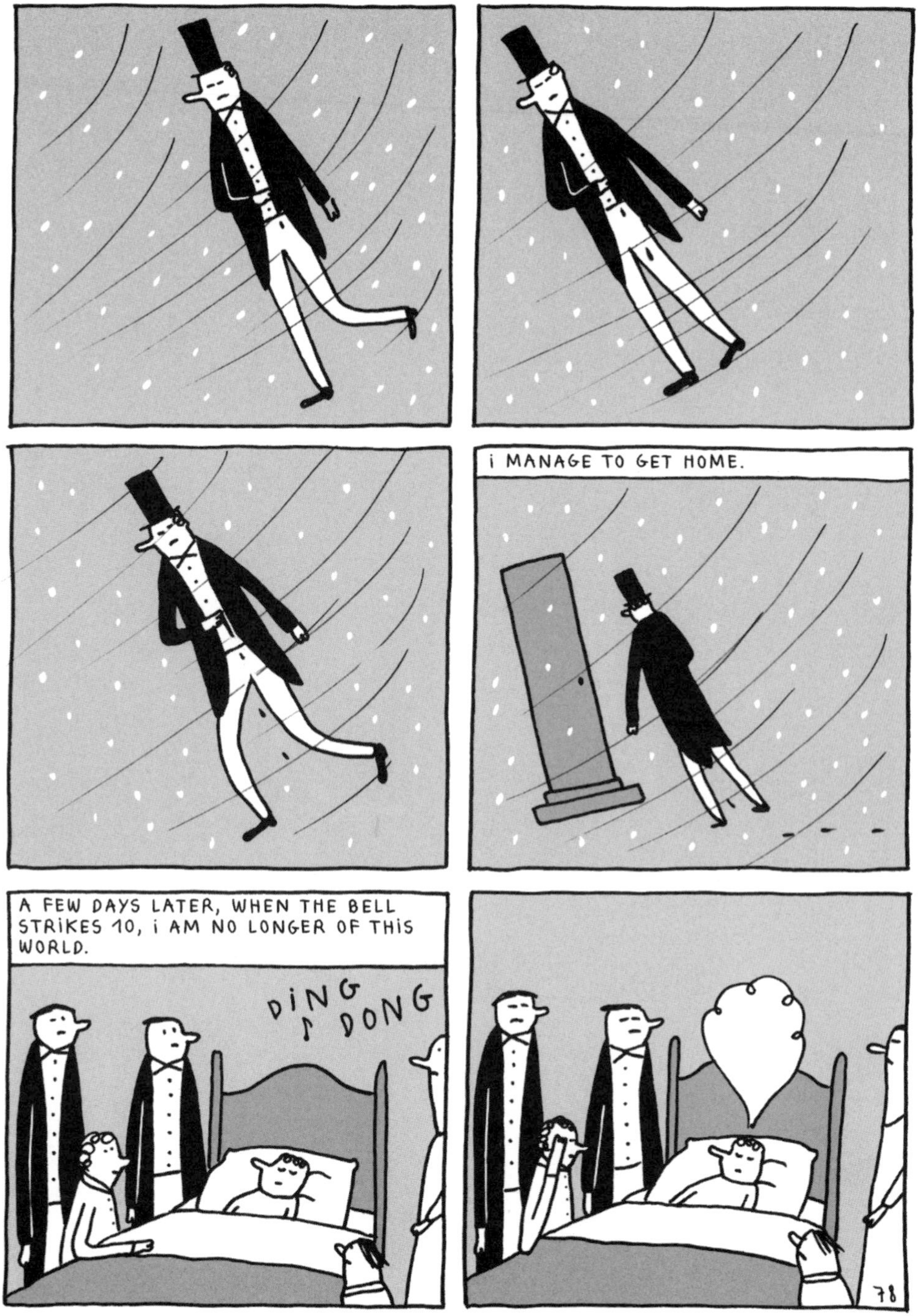
i MANAGE TO GET HOME.
A FEW DAYS LATER, WHEN THE BELL STRIKES 10, i AM NO LONGER OF THIS WORLD.
DiNG
DONG

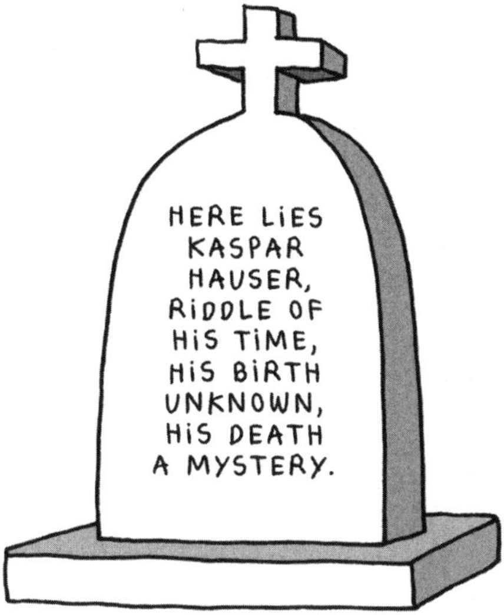
HERE LIES KASPAR HAUSER, RIDDLE OF HIS TIME, HIS BIRTH UNKNOWN, HIS DEATH A MYSTERY.

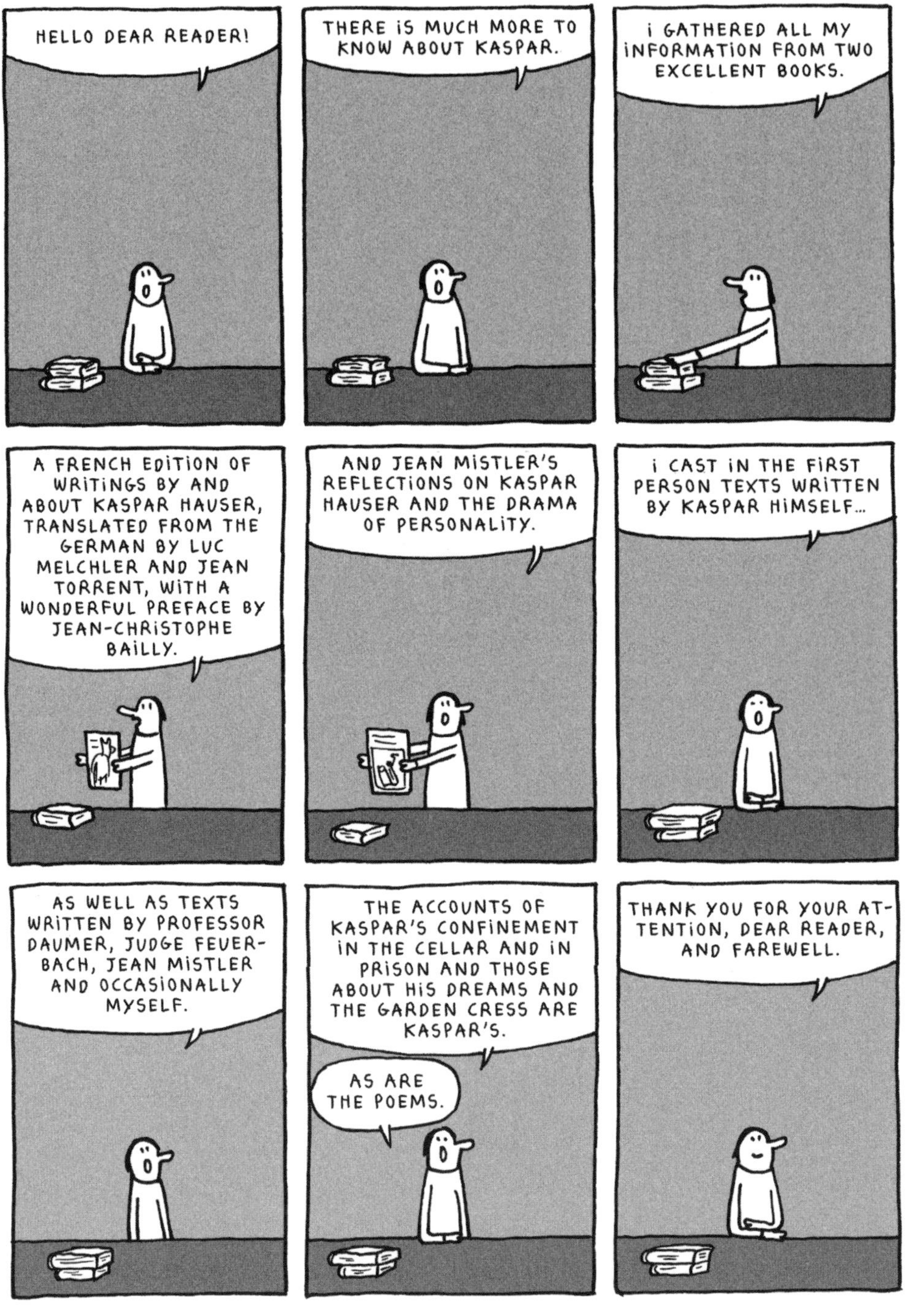
HELLO DEAR READER!
THERE IS MUCH MORE TO KNOW ABOUT KASPAR.
I GATHERED ALL MY INFORMATION FROM TWO EXCELLENT BOOKS.
A FRENCH EDITION OF WRITINGS BY AND ABOUT KASPAR HAUSER, TRANSLATED FROM THE GERMAN BY LUC MELCHLER AND JEAN TORRENT, WITH A WONDERFUL PREFACE BY JEAN-CHRISTOPHE BAILLY.
AND JEAN MISTLER'S REFLECTIONS ON KASPAR HAUSER AND THE DRAMA OF PERSONALITY.
I CAST IN THE FIRST PERSON TEXTS WRITTEN BY KASPAR HIMSELF...
AS WELL AS TEXTS WRITTEN BY PROFESSOR DAUMER, JUDGE FEUER-BACH, JEAN MISTLER AND OCCASIONALLY MYSELF.
THE ACCOUNTS OF KASPAR'S CONFINEMENT IN THE CELLAR AND IN PRISON AND THOSE ABOUT HIS DREAMS AND THE GARDEN CRESS ARE KASPAR'S.
AS ARE THE POEMS.
THANK YOU FOR YOUR AT-TENTION, DEAR READER, AND FAREWELL.

THE ENGLISH TRANSLATION OF KASPAR DRAWS ON THE
FOLLOWING ADDITIONAL SOURCES:

CATHERINE LUCY WILHELMINA POWLETT CLEVELAND, THE
LIFE AND LETTERS OF LADY HESTER STANHOPE, BY HER
NIECE; WITH A PREFATORY NOTE BY THE EARL OF ROSE-
BERY, LONDON: MURRAY, 1914; AND THE TRUE STORY OF
KASPAR HAUSER, FROM OFFICIAL DOCUMENTS, LONDON
AND NEW YORK: MACMILLAN AND CO., 1893.

PAUL JOHANN ANSELM FEUERBACH, CASPER HAUSER: AN
ACCOUNT OF AN INDIVIDUAL, KEPT IN A DUNGEON, SEPA-
RATED FROM ALL COMMUNICATION WITH THE WORLD,
FROM EARLY CHILDHOOD TO ABOUT THE AGE OF SEVEN-
TEEN: DRAWN UP FROM LEGAL DOCUMENTS: TO WHICH IS
ADDED A MEMOIR BY THE AUTHOR, TRANSLATED BY H.G.
LINBERG, LONDON: SIMPKIN AND MARSHALL, 1834.